Choose your Words

A School Thesaurus

Choose your Words

A School Thesaurus

by

C. Windridge

Ottenheimer Publishers, Inc.

Contents

Preface

Choose Your Words is a handy thesaurus for all students between 9 and 13 years of age. It provides for many of the important and immediate language needs of these students and is designed to become their invaluable companion. The students' attention should first be directed to the notes 'How to use this thesaurus' (page vii).

The book consists of a basic list of over two thousand commonly-used guide words (pages 9 to 115), carefully selected and arranged in alphabetical order. Alongside each guide word there is a group of synonyms and words that are similar in meaning. Occasionally, these groups contain words that have only a tenuous similarity in meaning to the relevant guide word, but may provide preferable alternatives: to this extent the author has used his considerable teaching experience to anticipate some of the errors frequently made by students. By using this section of the book, students will enlarge and enrich their vocabulary. It follows that they will develop their ability to speak or write more accurately or more stylishly and so express themselves more effectively.

The basic list of guide words is followed by a supplement which contains alphabetical lists of 'opposites' (pages 116 to 139)—some are true antonyms and some are approximately opposite in meaning but useful for the students to know and use. There are also separate pages of commonly-used archaic words (page 141) that the pupil will discover in literature and frequently-used foreign words and phrases (pages 142 and 143). The supplement also contains a set of simple instructions to assist in the formation of antonyms by using the appropriate affixes (page 140). Taken together, the words in the basic list and the words in the supplement provide the student with a wide choice of close to 20,000 words.

How to use this thesaurus

Please read the following notes carefully.

What is a thesaurus?

A thesaurus has the appearance and some of the qualities of a dictionary and it can be used as such on a limited scale. However, the essential difference between a dictionary and a thesaurus is this: in a dictionary you refer to words whose meanings are not known to you, or about which you are uncertain, and so become fully acquainted with their correct meanings, whereas in a thesaurus you refer to familiar words, whose meanings are already known to you, and thereby become aware of less familiar words with the same or similar meanings but which may be more suitable for your purpose.

Guide words

The first column contains an alphabetical list, in bold type, of many of the everyday words with which you should be familiar. These are the *guide words*. They are the words to which you refer. Guide words that are spelled the same but differ in meaning with pronunciation are dealt with as follows:

content   *a.* happy, pleased, glad, satisfied

content   *n.* filling, constituents, ingredients, capacity, volume

The underlining indicates the stressed syllable(s).

In general, only one part of speech is shown, e.g., **absent** (page 10), is shown as an adjective although it is also a verb. Exceptionally, more than one part of speech is shown where there is likely to be confusion or where the various parts of speech have different meanings, e.g., **abandon, abandoned** (page 9). If the word you have in mind is not listed in the guide words, then refer to another common word of the same meaning, e.g., **misuse** is not in the guide words, but *misuse* and the words of a similar meaning are to be found alongside **abuse** (page 10).

Abbreviations

The second column contains the abbreviations that are used to indicate the parts of speech. These abbreviations, which are in italics, are as follows:

a. adjective	*adv.* adverb	*conj.* conjunction	*int.* interjection
n. noun	*prep.* preposition	*pron.* pronoun	*v.* verb.

Synonyms and words of similar meaning

The third column contains *synonyms* (words that are identical in meaning), words that are similar in meaning and words that are only approximately similar in meaning. From these, you select the most suitable word for your purpose and, generally, this means the word that is the most accurate or the most stylish.

You must exercise great caution when selecting words, for words of a similar meaning cannot always be freely interchanged, e.g., **abolish** (page 9) is similar in meaning to *invalidate,* but *abolished* cannot be replaced by *invalidated* in this sentence: "Lincoln *abolished* slavery."

Quite often, a word that is only approximately similar in meaning to the guide word is the best alternative, e.g., *frequent* is not a synonym of **visit** (page 109), but *frequented* is preferable to *visited* in this sentence: "They *visited* a café." One assumes "visited a café" is intended to mean "visited a café quite often" and not "visited a café on one occasion only."

Some guide words have more than one meaning. In these cases, the words that follow the guide word are separately listed, and the lists are numbered, e.g., **abreast** (page 9).

Alternative spellings and additional information are given in parentheses, e.g.,
  abduct   *v.*   . . . steal (a child) (page 9).

A specimen sentence is provided where there is likely to be some doubt about the use of a word, e.g., **above** *a.* The **above** statement is correct (page 9).

The symbol / is used to save space and avoid repetition, e.g., **aboveboard** (page 9) means "without suspicion." It also means "without deceit" and "without deception." These alternatives are given as "without suspicion/deceit/deception."

Supplement

This section (pages 116 to 143) contains lists of *antonyms* (words that are directly opposite in meaning) and words that are almost opposite in meaning (pages 116 to 139), archaic words (page 141), and foreign words and phrases (pages 142 and 143).

Where a guide word is more than one part of speech or has more than one meaning, its opposites are separately listed, and the lists are numbered, e.g., **abandon** 1. keep, retain, hold, remain in, occupy, take over; 2. restraint, caution, care.

The section **Forming Opposites** (page 140) shows you how to form opposites, or antonyms, by using suitable affixes.

A a

aback   *adv.*   backward, backwards,
to the back, rearward,
rearwards, to the rear,
in reverse, behind
taken aback: *surprised,
amazed, astonished,
astounded, shocked*

abandon   *v.*   give up, surrender, yield,
relinquish, disown, leave,
depart from, quit, resign,
desert, forsake, vacate

                      n.   freedom, liberty,
no restraint, excitement,
rashness, recklessness,
carelessness, impulsiveness,
lust, licentiousness

abandoned   *a.*   1. given up, surrendered,
relinquished, disowned,
derelict, deserted,
forsaken, vacated, vacant,
unoccupied, empty
2. unrestrained, reckless,
rash, wanton, lustful,
licentious, carefree

abate   *v.*   decrease, reduce, diminish,
lessen, weaken, quiet,
cease, end, finish, terminate

abdomen   *n.*   belly, bowels, intestines

abduct   *v.*   kidnap, carry off by force,
take away, remove (a
person), steal (a child)

abhor   *v.*   hate, detest, loathe, dislike
intensely, regard with
disgust/distaste

abide   *v.*   1. dwell, stay, live, reside,
lodge, rest, remain, wait
2. suffer, put up with,
submit to, bear, endure,
stand, tolerate, accept

ability   *n.*   skill, talent, cleverness,
smartness, competence,
capability, ingenuity,
capacity, power

able   *a.*   skillful, talented, clever,
smart, competent, efficient,
capable, ingenious

abnormal   *a.*   unusual, odd, strange,
eccentric, queer, peculiar,
bizarre, irregular,
uncommon, extraordinary,
exceptional

aboard   *prep.* on, on to, on board, in,
into, inside

abolish   *v.*   do away with, end, finish,
terminate, destroy, quash,
invalidate, disallow, ban,
bar, make void, annul,
nullify, eliminate, remove

abound   *v.*   be rich in/in excess/infested
with/plentiful/well-stocked,
teem, overflow

about   *prep.* of, to do with, concerned
with, in regard to, in
connection with, relative to,
in relation to
                      adv.   round, around, all round,
approximately, nearly,
almost

above   *prep.* over, higher than,
on top of, superior to
                      adv.   overhead, on high, upstairs,
The sun is **above** us.
                      a.   The **above** statement is
correct.

aboveboard *a.*   fair, honest, just, true,
right, correct, proper,
upright, straight,
straightforward, sound,
without suspicion/deceit/
deception, open, undisguised

abreast   *a.*   1. side by side
They walked two or three
abreast.
2. up to date with,
in touch with, aware.
Do you keep **abreast** of
the times?

abroad   *adv.*   far away, in/to a foreign
land/another distant country

9

abrupt   *a.*   sudden, unexpected, violent, sharp, quick, hurried, hasty, short, precipitate, blunt, curt, cross, brusque, terse, tart, laconic

absent   *a.*   away, not in existence/present/here, lacking, abstracted in mind

absentminded   *a.*   inattentive, forgetful, unmindful, heedless, dreamy, not alert/vigilant/watchful, careless, unwary

absolute   *a.*   1. complete, full, utmost
2. without limit, unrestricted, perfect, real, true, great, pure, unlimited, independent, arbitrary

absorb   *v.*   take/suck in, soak/swallow, up, engross
He was **absorbed** in a book.

abstain   *v.*   refrain, avoid, not take part in/participate

abstract   *a.*   unreal, impractical, ideal, vague, abstruse, theoretical
          n.   summary, brief list, short account, essence
          v.   remove, take away, steal, disengage, separate, deduct, condense, summarize, shorten

absurd   *a.*   silly, ridiculous, foolish, puerile, not sensible, nonsensical, crazy, stupid, asinine, brainless, odd, strange, eccentric, preposterous, unreasonable, irrational, illogical

abundance   *n.*   plenty, wealth, riches, overflow, excess, large/ample stock/supply, generous amount, spate, proliferation

abundant   *a.*   plentiful, rich, in excess, overflowing, teeming, rank, luxuriant, pouring, prolific, well-stocked, copious, ample, substantial, adequate, generous, considerable, boundless, unrestricted, unlimited

abuse   *v.*   use wrongly, misuse, harm, damage, injure, mistreat, maltreat, ill-treat, treat badly
          n.   Litter is an **abuse** of the countryside.
          a.   *"You idiot"* are **abusive** words.

accelerate   *v.*   increase speed/motion/velocity/rate, move/go faster/quicker/swifter/more rapidly, speed up

accept   *v.*   take, receive, undertake, abide by, tolerate, agree to/with, allow, regard favorably, approve, believe

access   *n.*   way in, entrance, doorway, door, passage, channel, opening, inlet, ingress, approach

accident   *n.*   1. mishap, misfortune, ill fortune, unfortunate, occurrence, injury, calamity
2. unexpected event, unpredictable occurrence, chance

accommodate   *v.*   1. oblige, serve, suit, provide for, equip, supply, furnish
2. house, lodge, provide rooms/dwelling/home/shelter/quarters for

accompany   *v.*   go with, escort, guide, be a companion to, assist, help, aid, support

accomplice   *n.*   partner/helper/assistant in wrongdoing/crime, accessory

accomplish   *v.*   do, achieve, perform, manage, succeed in doing

account   *n.*   1. report, story, description
2. invoice, bill, financial statement/record
3. reason, cause, explanation
          v.   give reason, find cause, explain, be responsible

accumulate	*v.*	gather, collect, assemble, amass, save, hoard, store
accurate	*a.*	exact, precise, correct, true, truthful, honest, reliable, dependable
accuse	*v.*	blame, charge, put/lay blame/responsibility on, indict
achieve	*v.*	gain, win, get, obtain, acquire, attain, reach, carry out, perform, accomplish
acid	*a.*	acidic, vinegary, tart, sour, harsh, biting, severe, sharp
acknowledge	*v.*	admit, recognize, take notice of, accept, confess, declare, grant, own, allow, answer, greet, salute
acquaint	*v.*	make known to/aware of, inform of/about
acquire	*v.*	gain, obtain, get, receive, win, come to own/possess, take, annex, collect, glean, achieve, attain, procure
act	*n.*	1. deed, feat, accomplishment 2. part (of a stage play), performance
	v.	1. do, perform, behave, work, operate ,2. pretend, sham, feign, mimic, mime, simulate, deceive, be false
action	*n.*	1. act, deed, performance 2. activity, movement, motion, work 3. battle, conflict Soldiers die in **action.**
active	*a.*	quick-moving, quick, rapid, fast, swift, lively, alive, brisk, spry, sprightly, nimble, agile, vivacious, busy, industrious, hard-working, energetic, vigorous, effective
actual	*a.*	real, true, genuine, present, current, existing, established

acute	*a.*	1. sharp, pointed, not blunt An angle which contains less than 90° is **acute.** 2. high, penetrating, shrill 3. keen, sensitive, sharp, quick 4. severe, serious, critical, intense
adamant	*a.*	stubborn, firm, determined, unyielding, resolute, obdurate
adapt	*v.*	adjust, change, alter, fit, suit, remodel, modify The film was **adapted** from the novel.
address	*n.*	1. place, location 2. talk, speech, oration, discourse
	v.	1. I shall **address** the envelope. 2. give a talk to, make a speech to, orate/hold forth to, harangue
adequate	*a.*	sufficient, enough, ample, suitable, satisfactory, fit, proper
adhere	*v.*	stick, stick together, cling, attach
adhesive	*n.*	gum, glue, paste, cement, fixative, sticky substance, mucilage
	a.	Gum and molasses are **adhesive.**
adjacent	*a.*	next, side by side, alongside, near, near by, close, neighboring
adjust	*v.*	change, alter, adapt, arrange, regulate
admire	*v.*	respect, approve, like, appreciate, esteem, praise, applaud
admission	*n.*	admittance, entrance, access
admit	*v.*	accept, allow, grant, confess, declare, recognize, acknowledge
adopt	*v.*	choose, select, take, take over, accept

11

adore	*v.*	love, cherish, worship, admire, intensely, deify
adrift	*adv.*	drifting, untied, unmoored, free
adult	*a.*	mature, grown-up, fully-grown
advance	*v.*	1. progress, go forward, approach 2. offer, propose, make an overture She **advanced** a few hints. 3. lend, pay cash/money in advance He advanced her $14.50.
advantage	*n.*	1. help, aid, benefit, profit, gain 2. superiority, better position **take advantage:** *act unfairly*
adversary	*n.*	enemy, foe, opponent, rival, antagonist, contestant
advertise	*v.*	make known, make public, publicize
advice	*n.*	counsel, guidance, opinion given, news, information, notification, bulletin
affair	*n.*	matter, business, concern, event, occasion, incident
affect	*v.*	1. change, move, touch (emotionally) 2. pretend, act, assume, practice
	a.	The actress is vain and **affected**.
affection	*n.*	love, liking, fondness, tenderness, attachment, endearment
afford	*v.*	1. be able/have the means/be wealthy enough to buy/purchase, spare 2. supply, provide, give, furnish, bestow, yield
aflame	*a.*	in flame, flaming, alight, on fire, afire, aglow, glowing, ablaze, blazing, burning
afloat	*adv.*	floating, at sea, aboard ship, on board ship
afraid	*a.*	frightened, scared, alarmed, in fear, fearful, timid, uneasy, apprehensive
age	*n.*	1. long time, era, period 2. later life
	v.	grow/become older, develop
agent	*n.*	1. representative, deputy, steward, factor 2. force, cause, means
aggressive	*a.*	quarrelsome, belligerent, bellicose, warlike
agile	*a.*	nimble, lively, spry, athletic, active, quick-moving, brisk
agitate	*v.*	1. bother, disturb, excite, alarm, worry, fluster 2. stir, shake, move
agony	*n.*	great pain, anguish, torment, suffering
agree	*v.*	1. concur, approve, allow, accept, grant, share opinion, consent, concede 2. match, correspond, coincide
agreeable	*a.*	pleasant, pleasing, tasteful, inviting, well-disposed, satisfactory, willing/ready/prepared to accept, acceptable, in agreement
agreement	*n.*	1. promise, bargain, contract, bond, guarantee, warranty, covenant, treaty, truce, pact, pledge 2. accord, concord, mutual understanding
ahead	*adv.*	in advance, in front, before, forward
aid	*n.*	help, assistance, support
	v.	help, assist, succor, support
ailment	*n.*	illness, sickness, malady

aim	*n.*	purpose, intent, intention, object, objective, target, goal, ambition, end
	v.	1. intend, resolve
		2. take aim/a line on, direct, level, point (at a target)
air	*n.*	1. atmosphere
		2. appearance, manner, style
	v.	dry, warm, allow air to enter (room/clothes)
alarm	*n.*	1. warning, alert
		2. fear, fright, panic, excitement, agitation
	v.	1. warn, alert, make aware
		2. frighten, disturb, startle, excite, agitate
alert	*a.*	lively, alive, active, nimble, spry, attentive, wide-awake, wary, cautious, watchful, vigilant
	n.	alarm, warning
	v.	alarm, warn, make aware
alight	*a.*	lighted, on fire, burning, aflame, in flame
	v.	get down, descend, dismount, settle
alike	*a.*	like, similar, akin
	adv.	similarly, in like matter
allow	*v.*	1. let, permit, consent/agree to, tolerate, accept, abide by, put up with, stand, suffer, bear, award, give, grant, bestow
		2. admit, own, agree, concede, concur, confess, declare, acknowledge, recognize
almost	*adv.*	nearly, all but
aloft	*adv.*	above, overhead, high up, upward
alone	*a.*	lone, lonely, solitary
	adv.	only, exclusively
also	*adv.*	too, besides, in addition, additionally, as well, furthermore, moreover, what is more

alter	*v.*	change, vary, modify, adjust, rearrange, remodel, redesign, adapt, convert, transform
altogether	*adv.*	entirely, wholly, on the whole, totally, in total, completely, fully
amateur	*n.*	beginner, novice, nonprofessional
amaze	*v.*	surprise, astonish, astound, fill with wonder, overwhelm, shock, flabbergast, dumbfound
ambition	*n.*	desire, hope, aspiration, aim, target, goal, object, objective
amend	*v.*	correct, put right, make better, better, reform, improve
amiable	*a.*	friendly, agreeable, amicable, good-natured, well-disposed, of good humor, good-tempered, even-tempered, pleasant, likeable, lovable
among	*prep.*	amongst, amid, amidst
amount	*n.*	1. quality, number, total
		2. cost, total cost, full value
	v.	The bill **amounts** to $8.96.
ample	*a.*	enough sufficient, adequate, more than enough, generous, substantial, abundant, plentiful, rich, copious
amuse	*v.*	entertain, cause laughter, make laugh, be comical/ funny, divert, entertain, beguile
anger	*n.*	rage, annoyance, wrath, ire, temper, vexation, fury, irritation
angle	*n.*	1. corner, sharp, bend/turn, point
		2. approach, aspect, slant, viewpoint, standpoint

animal	*n.*	beast, brute, creature **animals**: *creatures, animal-life, fauna*
announce	*v.*	make known, tell, declare, report, reveal, advertise, broadcast, proclaim, publish, notify
annoy	*v.*	anger, enrage, exasperate, harass, aggravate, irritate, bother, pester, molest, badger
annual	*a.*	yearly
	n.	A marigold plant is an **annual**.
anonymous	*a.*	nameless, unknown
another	*a.*	one more, a different, an additional
	pron.	additional one
answer	*n.*	1. solution, result 2. reply, retort
anticipate	*v.*	expect, hope, predict, forestall, use in advance, look forward to, realize/consider beforehand, accelerate
anxiety	*n.*	worry, concern, disquiet, uneasiness, trouble, anguish
apart	*adv.*	aside, separately, independently, asunder **set apart**: *put aside/on one side, reserve, devote*
apparel	*n.*	dress, clothing, attire, garments, garb
apparent	*a.*	seen, clear, plain, obvious, probable, likely
appeal	*v.*	request, beg, ask, pray, plead, entreat, implore, beseech
appear	*v.*	1. become apparent/visible, come into sight/view, materialize 2. look, seem
applaud	*v.*	praise, laud, clap hands, cheer, shout for, acclaim, commend
apply	*v.*	1. ask, request, make an application 2. attend, commit, devote, engage
appreciation	*n.*	1. estimation, judgement, understanding, perception, recognition, approval, admiration 2. rise/growth/increase in value
approach	*n.*	1. way to/in, access, entrance 2. advance, overture, offer, proposal
	v.	near, go closer to, come towards
appropriate	*a.*	correct, right, proper, suitable, becoming, fit, fitting, befitting, apt, apposite, well put/said/chosen, relevant, adequate
appropriate	*v.*	take possession of, steal, annex, confiscate
approve	*v.*	accept, like, esteem, allow, permit, sanction, assent/consent to, agree to/with, confirm, commend
apt	*a.*	1. suitable, appropriate, fit, fitting, befitting, becoming 2. witty, quick-witted, smart, clever, apposite, well put/chosen (remark)
argue	*v.*	differ, dispute, discuss, debate, prove, reason, maintain, indicate
arms	*n.*	1. weapons 2. upper limbs (of humans), branches, outgrowths, projections, crosspieces
aroma	*n.*	sweet smell/scent/odor/essence, perfume, fragrance
arouse	*v.*	awaken, waken, rouse, bestir, stir into action/activity, stimulate

arrange	*v.*	1. order, group, sort, select, adjust 2. plan, prepare, organize
arrest	*v.*	1. stop, halt, check, apprehend 2. catch, hold, grasp, take prisoner, secure, capture, seize
art	*n.*	skill, craft, technique, knack, trade, aesthetic activity
artful	*a.*	cunning, crafty, sly, wily, deceitful, devious
article	*n.*	1. object, item, thing, ware 2. account, description, extract
ascend	*v.*	rise, go/get/come up, scale, slope upwards
ashamed	*a.*	abashed, guilt-conscious, aware of disgrace, embarrassed
ask	*v.*	1. request, invite, call for, demand, require, want, need 2. inquire, question, call for an answer **ask after:** *inquire about (a person)*
assault	*n.*	violent attack/advance, onslaught, charge, rape
assemble	*v.*	1. fit/put/join together, build, construct, erect, compile, combine 2. gather, together, congregate, collect, meet, convene, throng, group, muster, rally
assist	*v.*	help, aid, succor, support
associate	*v.*	join, join together/in mix, partner, affiliate, relate to
assortment	*n.*	mixture, collection, variety, selection
assume	*v.*	suppose, pretend, act, simulate, take for granted, take upon, undertake
assure	*v.*	convince, give confidence to, guarantee, make sure/safe/certain, tell with confidence
astonish	*v.*	astound, surprise, amaze, shock, overwhelm, fill with wonder, flabbergast, dumbfound
astound	*v.*	astonish, surprise, amaze, shock, overwhelm, make wonder, flabbergast, dumbfound
astray	*adv.*	off course, wandering, out of the way **gone astray:** *lost, mislaid*
attach	*v.*	fasten, fix, affix, connect, combine, join, unite, bind, marry, tie
attachment	*n.*	bond, devotion, friendship, affection, love, fondness, endearment
attack	*n.*	1. bout, spell, turn, fit, spasm, sudden occurrence 2. assault, onslaught, battle
	v.	assault, fall upon, do battle with, storm charge
attain	*v.*	achieve, accomplish, gain, get, obtain, win, earn, reach, arrive at, come to
attempt	*n.*	try, trial, endeavor, essay
attend	*v.*	1. be present at, go regularly to 2. escort guide, accompany, serve, wait upon, help, assist, aid support 3. heed, take notice, give thought/attention/care/consideration/application, show interest
attire	*n.*	dress, clothing, apparel, garments, garb, costume
attract	*v.*	draw to/towards, bring near, influence, please, excite, entice, lure, charm
audacity	*n.*	boldness, forwardness, pertness, sauciness, cheek, impudence, impertinence

audience	*n.*	1. listeners, spectators, assembly, gathering 2. interview, hearing
authentic	*a.*	real, true, genuine, of undoubted origin, trustworthy, reliable
authority	*n.*	power, right, rule, control, command, influence, administration, government
avail	*v.*	help, be of value/profit, benefit
available	*a.*	near, handy, within reach, on supply, supplied
avarice	*n.*	greed, love of wealth/riches/possessions, possessiveness
average	*a.*	normal, usual, standard, common, ordinary, medium, mean, mediocre
aversion	*n.*	dislike, distaste, antipathy, loathing, abhorrence
avert	*v.*	avoid, prevent, ward off, turn away
avoid	*v.*	escape, avert, shun, dodge, refrain/abstain/keep away from, elude
await	*v.*	wait for, expect, anticipate, be kept for A letter and a parcel **await** you.
awake	*v.*	awaken, wake, wake up, arouse, rouse, rouse up, bestir
aware	*a.*	conscious, knowing, cognizant, well-informed, wary, watchful, vigilant, wide-awake, mindful
away	*adv.*	1. at/to a distance, another place, off, aside, apart, absent, not present 2. constantly, continuously, on and on, all the time The gardener works **away** with his spade
awe	*n.*	wonder, respect, reverence, fear
awkward	*a.*	clumsy, bungling, unskillful, gawky, ungainly, ill-adapted, difficult, not easy, risky, embarrassing

B b

babble   *v.*   prattle, gab, gabble, jabber, gibber, chatter, speak unintelligibly/confusedly/ excessively/foolishly/ babyishly, be inarticulate/ incoherent, talk idly

            n.   prattle, idle talk, babytalk

babyish   *a.*   infantile, childish, immature, silly

back   *n.*   rear, hinder part, reverse side

            v.   1. support, assist, help

                  2. go back/backwards, reverse

                  3. bet/gamble/wager/stake on

backward   *a.*   1. slow, behindhand, retarded, dull, unintelligent, obtuse, reluctant, reticent, shy

                  2. reversed, in reverse

           adv.   backwards, rearward, rearwards, behind, aback

bad   *a.*   1. naughty, badly-behaved, unruly, disobedient, ill-mannered, rude, wrong, evil, malevolent, immoral, vile, sinful, vicious, vindictive, malignant, corrupt, depraved, base, lustful, profligate, licentious

                  2. poor, lacking in quality, faulty, defective, blemished, unpleasant, distasteful, noxious, harmful, debased, tainted, unwholesome, adulterated, decayed, rotten, putrefied

                  3. ill, sick, ailing, not well, unwell, poorly, indisposed

badge   *n.*   mark, sign, symbol, emblem, device, token, crest

badger   *v.*   bully, browbeat, threaten, worry, bother, tease, torment, persecute

baffle   *v.*   mystify, bewilder, perplex, hoax, puzzle, confuse, confound, deceive, mislead, elude, hinder

baggage   *n.*   bags, cases, luggage, belongings

bait   *v.*   worry, bother, trouble, anger, annoy, browbeat, heckle, tease, torment, cause to bite

            n.   lure (in a trap or on a fish-hook), enticement

balance   *v.*   weigh, make equal, equate, match, equalize, keep in equilibrium, counterpoise, neutralize, waver, oscillate

            n.   1. poise, equilibrium, neutrality

                  2. scales, weighing-machine

ball   *n.*   1. sphere, spheroid, globe, globule, orb, shot

                  2. dance, social gathering

ban   *v.*   forbid, bar, not permit/allow, disallow, quash, annul, nullify, disqualify, put/make an end to, make void, reject, prohibit

band   *n.*   1. group, gang, company, troop, pack, flock, herd

                  2. strip, stripe, border, bar, collar, ribbon

bandit   *n.*   brigand, robber, outlaw, criminal, crook, gangster, ruffian, highwayman, mugger

bang   *n.*   1. loud noise/sound, burst, explosion, report, crash

                  2. bump, thump, blow, knock, thud

17

banish	*v.*	exile, send away, remove from, oust, cast out, outlaw
bar	*v.*	forbid, ban, not permit/allow, disallow, disqualify, reject
	n.	1. beam, girder, rod, pole, barrier, counter, barricade
		2. strip, stripe, line, band
bare	*a.*	naked, bald, uncovered, unclothed, unfurnished, undisguised, unadorned, empty, scanty, meager
barely	*adv.*	merely, only just, scarcely, almost, nearly, not quite
barren	*a.*	fruitless, infertile, empty, dull, unprofitable, worthless
barrier	*n.*	bar, barricade, gate, fence, hedge, obstacle, blockade, obstruction, hindrance
base	*n.*	bottom, foot, foundation, pedestal, support
	a.	low, vulgar, despicable, despised, contemptible, mean, selfish, cowardly, immoral, worthless, ignoble, corrupt, depraved, vile
bashful	*a.*	shy, easily embarrassed, shamefaced, sheepish
basis	*n.*	1. principle, foundation, grounds
		2. main/chief part/ portion/ingredient
battle	*n.*	conflict, encounter, fray, fight, struggle, combat, strife, skirmish, action
beam	*n.*	1. bar, girder, crosspiece, plank, lever, rod
		2. ray/shaft of light/ electromagnetic waves
bear	*v.*	1. carry, support, hold, uphold, transport, yield, produce
		2. suffer, endure, abide, put up with, stand, tolerate
		bear out: *confirm, substantiate, warrant, guarantee*
beast	*n.*	animal, brute, creature, quadruped, savage
beautiful	*a.*	fair, lovely, pretty, handsome, good-looking, beauteous, attractive, delightful, charming, splendid, fine, enchanting
become	*v.*	1. change to/into, commence/begin to be
		2. suit, befit, adorn
becoming	*a.*	suitable, fitting, befitting, appropriate
before	*adv.*	in front/advance, ahead, earlier, beforehand, already, preceding
befriend	*v.*	be a friend to, be friendly with, accept as a friend, aid, assist, help, favor
beg	*v.*	ask for, request, implore, plead, entreat, beseech, pray, appeal to, exhort
beggarly	*a.*	1. very small, little, slight, trifling, mean, meager, inadequate
		2. poor, shabby, sordid, vagrant
begin	*v.*	commence, start, take the first step, go/set to work
behave	*v.*	act, act properly/ correctly/with propriety/ with courtesy/with discretion/mannerly
behind	*adv.*	behindhand, in arrears, in/to the rear, backward, at/to the back/rear, back, after, afterwards, late, belated, retarded
belief	*n.*	knowledge, faith, trust, confidence, thought, opinion, intuition
belly	*n.*	abdomen, bowels, intestines **belly-ache:** *stomach-ache, abdominal pains, colic*
belong	*v.*	be attached/situated/sited, be part/the business/the concern/the property of, apply, pertain, appertain, be associated with

belongings	*n.*	personal property, baggage, luggage
below	*adv.*	under, underneath, beneath, at/to a lower level, downstairs, downstream, in hell
	prep.	at/to a greater depth than, lower/lesser than (in size, position, rank or degree)
bend	*v.*	turn, curve, twist, make/become angular, incline
beneath	*prep.*	inferior to, not worthy of
benefit	*n.*	advantage, gain, profit, help, aid, assistance, favor, allowance, pension, privilege, "perk"
benevolent	*a.*	kindly, helpful, magnanimous, big-hearted, generous, bountiful, munificent, charitable, well-disposed, ready to help, philanthropic
beside	*prep.*	close to, near, by, on/at a level with, alongside, adjacent to
best	*a.*	of the most excellent kind, in the most excellent way, finest, most suitable/ appropriate/fitting
bestial	*a.*	beast-like, brutish,. brutal, cruel, bloodthirsty, wild, savage, barbarous, obscene
bet	*v.*	put/place a bet on, back, stake, wager, gamble
better	*a.*	improved, amended, superior, preferable, more desirable
	v.	improve, amend, surpass
betterment	*n.*	improvement, advancement, welfare
bewilder	*v.*	mystify, baffle, puzzle, perplex, confuse

beyond	*prep.*	out of reach of, on/at the farther side of, past, outside
	adv.	at a distance, yonder, past, outside
	n.	the unknown, future life, most distant/remote part of the earth
bicker	*v.*	quarrel, differ, dispute, argue, wrangle
bid	*v.*	1. offer, invite, proclaim, announce
		2. greet, salute, acknowledge I **bid** you goodnight.
		3. order, command, instruct
big	*a.*	large, great, grand, huge, giant, gigantic, vast, immense, tremendous, enormous, enlarged, swollen, impressive, important, serious, momentous
bill	*n.*	1. invoice, account, statement of account
		2. notice, poster, placard, program, menu
		handbill: *printed notice, leaflet*
bind	*v.*	join, unite, fasten, hold/tie together, marry
bit	*n.*	small piece/part/portion/ fraction, fragment, morsel, chip, splinter
bite	*v.*	nip, sting, wound (with teeth), grip
bitter	*a.*	not sweet, biting, harsh, unrelenting, relentless, virulent, extremely/ piercingly cold, resentful, disappointed
blame	*v.*	accuse, find fault with, charge, lay fault/trouble on, put responsibility on
blank	*a.*	empty, vacant, not written/ printed on
blatant	*a.*	noisy, loud-voiced, clamorous, flagrant, palpable, undisguised, open, obvious

19

blaze	*n.*	bright flame/fire/light/illumination
bleak	*a.*	dreary, drab, dull, uninteresting, bare, exposed, windswept, chilly, austere
blemish	*n.*	defect, error, flaw, stain, bad quality, injury
	v.	taint, mar, sully, spoil the beauty/quality of
blend	*v.*	mix, mingle, become one, unite, merge, match, harmonize
blessed	*a.*	holy, consecrated, sacred, sacrosanct, revered, fortunate, lucky, well-favored, blissful
blind	*a.*	1. without sight, sightless, unseeing 2. unknowing, not aware, unaware, without discernment/foresight/understanding/appreciation
block	*v.*	stop, obstruct, wedge, fill up, oppose, hinder
bloodthirsty	*a.*	desirous of/eager for/wanting bloodshed, cruel, brutal, bestial, wild, savage, barbarous
blossom	*n.*	bloom, flower, inflorescence
blot	*n.*	spot, stain, mark, dark patch, blemish, disfigurement
blow	*n.*	1. knock, hit, stroke, bang, jab, buffet, cuff, punch, rap, tap 2. shock, mishap, misfortune, bad/ill luck, disaster, calamity, loss, bad news 3. puff, pant, gasp, gust
bluff	*a.*	abrupt, outspoken, frank, candid, blunt, sincere, genial, cordial, vigorous, abundant
	n.	deception, pretense, idle/empty threat
blunder	*v.*	1. make/commit a mistake/error/indiscretion, mismanage/mishandle a situation 2. move/walk clumsily/blindly, act/behave awkwardly, stumble, trip, fall over
	n.	mistake, error, oversight, indiscretion, foolish/stupid/silly/compromising/embarrassing act/conduct, *faux pas*
blurred	*a.*	indistinct, obscure, dim, not clear, hazy, misty, nebulous, confused, sullied, disfigured, smeared, stained, blemished, marked
boast	*n.*	brag, vanity, vainglory, pride, bombast, swagger, pretension
	v.	brag, vaunt, exaggerate, swank
body	*n.*	1. trunk, torso, physique, figure, frame, form, anatomy 2. corpse, cadaver, remains 3. mass, amount, quantity, group, company, crowd, association, organization, corporation
bog	*n.*	marsh, morass, mire, quagmire, swamp, slough, fen
bogus	*a.*	false, fictitious, sham, forged, counterfeit
bold	*a.*	forward, saucy, cheeky, pert, impertinent, impudent, audacious, brave, daring, reckless, not afraid, fearless, courageous, determined, resolute
bond	*n.*	1. joint, union, knot, tie, link, marriage 2. agreement, contract, promise to pay
bondage	*n.*	slavery, serfdom, servitude, imprisonment, confinement, restraint, subjection

bonus	n.	goodwill payment, extra payment/dividend/ distribution, gratuity, something beneficial/to the good/into the bargain
booty	n.	plunder, loot, profit, gain, reward, prize, treasure
border	n.	edge, margin, division, dividing/demarcation line, boundary, frontier
bore	v.	1. drill, pierce, make a hole 2. be tiresome/wearisome, uninteresting/a nuisance
	n.	hole, diameter (of a hole), caliber (of a gun)
borrow	v.	take/obtain a loan, adopt, derive
bottle	n.	flask, carafe, flagon, jar, vial, phial, vessel
bough	n.	branch, arm
bound	n.	1. leap, jump, spring, gambol 2. limit, boundary
boundless	a.	without limit, unlimited, limitless, endless, infinite
bout	n.	1. spell/turn of work/ exercise, attack/fit of illness/drinking, spasm, sudden occurrence 2. trial of strength, contest, battle, fight, conflict
bowels	n.	intestines, belly, abdomen, lower part of body
boycott	v.	shun, ignore, avoid, disregard, eschew, cold-shoulder
branch	n.	bough, arm, limb, tributary, outgrowth, projection, line, subdivision
brat	n.	urchin, naughty/ mischievous/roguish child
bravado	n.	defiance, show/display of bravery/courage, pretended bravery/boldness

brave	a.	courageous, bold, daring, dashing, fearless, plucky, valiant, valorous, dauntless, undaunted, heroic, gallant
brawl	v.	quarrel, squabble, fight
brawny	a.	muscular, strong, powerful, vigorous
break	v.	fracture, crack, shatter, splinter, sever, split, damage **break down:** *fall, collapse, demolish, decompose, analyze* **break in/into:** *enter, breach* **break up:** *dismiss, disintegrate, decay, decompose*
brief	a.	short, concise, not long, succinct, terse, summarized, laconic
bright	a.	1. shining, gleaming, brilliant, radiant, lustrous, glowing, lit up, glossy 2. clever, smart, intelligent, quick-witted, alert, talented, vivacious
brilliant	a.	1. bright, shining, gleaming, lustrous, sparkling, twinkling, scintillating 2. very clever/intelligent/ talented/gifted, illustrious
bring	v.	carry to/from, bear, convey, transport, fetch, lead, guide **bring about/to pass:** *cause to happen/occur* **bring down:** *abase, ruin, wound, kill, destroy* **bring to mind:** *recall, recollect, remember*
brink	n.	edge, border, brim
brisk	a.	quick, quick-moving, rapid, fast, lively, energetic, vigorous, keen, enlivening, stimulating
brittle	a.	fragile, breakable, apt/liable to break, easily broken/fractured, frail, delicate, weak

broad	*a.*	wide, not narrow, extensive, expansive, comprehensive, all-embracing, complete, open, full, clear, explicit, main, large
broadcast	*v.*	distribute, scatter, sow, disseminate, transmit, announce, advertise
	n.	radio/television transmission
browse	*v.*	1. graze, nibble
		2. read fitfully/without concentration
brutal	*a.*	bestial, beastly, cruel, savage, wild, barbarous, depraved, obscene
build	*v.*	put up, put/fit together, assemble, erect, construct, make, manufacture, fabricate, fashion, establish, institute, develop
bulk	*n.*	size, amount, quantity, capacity, volume, mass, main part/portion/fraction, contents
bully	*v.*	browbeat, bluster, threaten, badger, bother, pester, persecute, oppress, hector
bump	*n.*	1. noise, sound, bang, thud
		2. thump, blow, rap, hit, stroke, jolt

bumptious	*a.*	conceited, vain, self-opinionated, self-centered, proud, egotistical, boastful, bombastic
bunch	*n.*	cluster, small group, knot, handful
burden	*n.*	1. load, weight, capacity
		2. worry, problem, anxiety, responsibility
burn	*v.*	set on fire, blaze, flame, ignite, incinerate, consume (by fire), cremate
burst	*v.*	fly/split apart/open, explode, collapse, disintegrate
business	*n.*	1. matter, affair, agenda
		2. task, job, work, trade, commerce, employment, occupation, profession, vocation
busy	*a.*	active, fully occupied, working, employed, engaged, diligent
		busybody: *fussy/ interfering/meddlesome person*
butcher	*v.*	kill, slaughter, slay, murder, massacre
buy	*v.*	purchase
bystander	*n.*	onlooker, spectator, eyewitness, witness

C c

café — *n.* — coffee-shop, tea-shop, - restaurant

calculate — *v.* — work out, estimate, determine, assess, reckon, compute

call — *v.* —
1. shout, cry, hail, greet
2. name, address as, know as
3. summon, invite, send for
4. proclaim, announce, signal

call on: *visit*

calm — *a.* — gentle, peaceful, quiet, easy, relaxed, composed, serene, placid, unruffled, matter of fact, undisturbed, still, windless

camouflage — *v.* — disguise, hide, conceal, cover, mask

cancel — *v.* — cross out, delete, erase, remove, withdraw

capable — *a.* — able, efficient, skillful, proficient, competent, clever, talented, qualified

capital — *a.* —
1. chief, main, principal, largest, leading
2. fine, excellent, splendid, superb

n. —
1. main/chief city
2. assets, wealth

capsize — *v.* — overturn, tip over, upset

captain — *n.* — company-commander (army), leader, chief, head, commander of ship/aircraft, master, skipper

capture — *a.* — catch, seize, arrest, trap, snare, ensnare, grasp, grab, take, get

car — *n.* — motorcar, automobile, vehicle, carriage

care — *n.* —
1. attention, interest, regard, consideration, trouble, pains
2. concern, worry, anxiety
3. caution, watchfulness, prudence, vigilance, wariness

career — *n.* — profession, vocation, calling, development, progress

v. — run/go swiftly/wildly

careless — *a.* — uncaring, thoughtless, heedless, not careful/ cautious/prudent, imprudent, incautious, unmindful

cargo — *n.* — goods, freight, load, shipment

carry — *v.* — fetch, convey, transport, transfer

case — *v.* — enclose, cover, contain

n. —
1. container, box, holder, crate
2. event, occurrence, matter, business, example, instance
3. lawsuit, action

cash — *n.* — money, coins, currency, funds

cast — *v.* —
1. throw, pitch, toss, heave, fling
2. drop, shed, let fall
3. mould, shape, form

n. — actors, performers

casual — *a.* — easygoing, not arranged, informal, incautious, uncaring, negligent, careless

catch — *v.* — grasp, hold, seize, get, grip, capture, take, arrest, trap, snare, ensnare

catch up with: *draw level with*

cause	*n.*	reason, purpose, start, beginning, origin
	v.	make happen/occur, force, compel
cautious	*a.*	careful, heedful, mindful, watchful, vigilant, prudent, wary
cease	*v.*	stop, end, finish, conclude, terminate
ceaseless	*a.*	without ceasing/ending, unceasing, incessant, never-ending, constant
celebrate	*v.*	make merry, be festive, rejoice, observe, keep, honor, praise, laud, applaud
center	*n.*	middle, midpoint, midst, core, heart, kernel
ceremony	*n.*	solemn/stately/formal celebration/occasion/ function/custom/ performance, rite
certain	*a.*	1. sure, definite, without doubt 2. particular, specific
challenge	*n.*	dare, defy, question, oppose, contend
champion	*n.*	1. victor, winner 2. defender, supporter, protector
	a.	unbeaten, unequalled, unsurpassed, best, supreme
chance	*n.*	1. risk, gamble 2. luck, fortune, fate, accident
change	*v.*	alter, substitute, adjust, vary, modify, convert, transform
chaos	*n.*	disorder, confusion, panic, turmoil, tumult
character	*n.*	1. nature, quality, type, sort, caliber, disposition 2. reputation 3. person (in a story, play or film)

charge	*n.*	1. attack, onslaught, stampede, rush 2. accusation, indictment 3. price, cost, amount, expense **in charge:** *responsible*
charm	*v.*	1. please, delight, attract, entice, captivate 2. bewitch, enchant, entrance
	n.	good luck/lucky token/trinket, magic, spell
chart	*n.*	map, plan, diagram
chat	*v.*	talk, converse, gossip, chatter
cheap	*a.*	inexpensive, not dear/costly, of little value, low-priced
cheat	*v.*	deceive, trick, dupe, swindle, defraud
	n.	swindler, trickster, fraud
check	*v.*	1. slow down, hinder, impede, retard, stop, arrest, halt 2. test, examine, inspect, investigate 3. rebuke, reprove
cheek	*n.*	audacity, impudence, impertinence, sauce
cheer	*v.*	1. please, gladden, hearten, encourage 2. applaud, shout for
chest	*n.*	1. breast, bosom, thorax 2. box, case, crate
chew	*v.*	masticate, grind, crunch, gnaw
chief	*a.*	main, principal, head, most important, largest, leading
	n.	chieftain, head, director, leader, captain
child	*n.*	infant, baby, minor
chill	*v.*	cool, make cold, refrigerate
	a.	frigid, cold, chilly, unemotional, unfeeling
	n.	feverish shivering, cold

chip	*n.*	tiny piece/part/chunk, splinter, fragment
choke	*v.*	smother, strangle, asphyxiate
choose	*v.*	opt, pick, prefer, favor, select, elect
chop	*v.*	cut, hack, incise, chip, slash, hew
chore	*n.*	task, job, menial duty
chum	*n.*	friend, companion, mate, comrade
civil	*a.*	courteous, polite, well-mannered, gracious
claim	*v.*	demand, ask for
clamp	*v.*	clasp, grip, brace
clash	*v.*	1. collide 2. contrast, produce disharmony, differ 3. disagree, dispute, quarrel
clasp	*v.*	clamp, grip, embrace, grasp, buckle, clutch, grab, snatch, hold
class	*n.*	group, set, category, grade, kind, sort, type, arrangement, selection
clean	*v.*	free from/remove dirt, wash, tidy, disinfect
	a.	not dirty, unsoiled, pure
clear	*a.*	1. plain, distinct, bright, cloudless, transparent, apparent, obvious 2. open, without hindrance/obstacles
clever	*a.*	intelligent, talented, skillful, ingenious, smart, bright, wise, shrewd, resourceful, adroit
climb	*v.*	ascend, mount, go/come up, scale
cling	*v.*	hold, clasp, clutch, stick, adhere
cloak	*n.*	1. coat, mantle, shawl, wrap 2. pretense, cover, concealment, disguise, mask
close	*v.*	1. shut, seal, cover 2. end, conclude, finish, terminate, complete
cloth	*n.*	fabric, material, textile
clothe	*v.*	dress, attire, garb, cover
clothing	*n.*	clothes, garments, attire, apparel, garb, dress, costume
clown	*n.*	jester, fool, buffoon, idiot, joker
club	*n.*	1. stick, cudgel, truncheon, bat, baton 2. society, group, circle, association
clue	*n.*	hint, guide, lead, key, suggestion, indication, inkling
clumsy	*a.*	awkward, ungainly, bungling, unskilled, not skillful, ungraceful
clutch	*v.*	hold, embrace, grab, seize, snatch, clasp, clamp, grip, grasp
coach	*n.*	1. carriage, car 2. teacher, instructor, tutor, trainer
	v.	teach, train, instruct
coarse	*a.*	1. not smooth, rough, matte, harsh, jagged 2. vulgar, common, uncouth, boorish, loutish, ill-mannered
coat	*n.*	jacket, garment, cover, covering, film, layer, fur, hair, wool
coax	*v.*	encourage, persuade, entice, tempt, wheedle, cajole
code	*n.*	1. system, pattern 2. secret signs/signals/words 3. set of rules/regulations/laws
coil	*n.*	spiral, helix
	v.	wind, turn, encircle, wrap around

cold	*a.*	1. chilly, cool, icy, freezing, frozen, frigid, wintry 2. distant, unfeeling, unemotional, cold-blooded 3. chill, feverish, shivering
collapse	*v.*	break down, fall, fall down, give way, cave in
collect	*v.*	gather, pick, store, assemble, bring together
collide	*v.*	meet, hit, crash, smash
color	*n.*	dye, paint, pigment, shade, hue, tint, stain
colossal	*a.*	gigantic, huge, massive, enormous, immense, tremendous, vast
combat	*n.*	fight, battle, encounter, struggle, action, fray, contest, engagement
combine	*v.*	join, unite, cooperate, blend, merge, mix
come	*v.*	arrive, advance, draw near, happen, occur
comfort	*n.* *v.*	ease, luxury, contentment console, sympathize with, cheer up, hearten, soothe
comic	*a.*	comical, funny, amusing, laughable, humorous, facetious, droll
command	*v.*	control, direct, take charge of, order, bid, instruct, require, rule, regulate, dictate
commence	*v.*	begin, start, initiate, instigate
commit	*v.*	1. do, perform, act 2. entrust, consign, send, deliver
common	*a.*	ordinary, commonplace, plain, vulgar, normal, standard, usual, everyday, average, cheap, widespread, well-known, customary, public
companion	*n.*	friend, comrade, chum, pal, mate
company	*n.*	1. group, assembly, gathering, band, gang, crew, troop, party, contingent 2. firm, business, syndicate 3. friends, companions, visitors
compare	*v.*	liken, be similar/alike, match, balance, harmonize
compel	*v.*	force, make, drive, press
compete	*v.*	strive, vie, participate, contest, struggle
competent	*a.*	able, capable, efficient, skilled, qualified, fit, suited
complain	*v.*	grumble, express discontent/dissatisfaction/displeasure, protest, nag
complete	*v.* *a.*	finish, end, conclude, close, terminate whole, full, total, entire, comprehensive, perfect, absolute
compliment	*v.*	praise, congratulate
compose	*v.*	1. put together, compile, form, create, invent, originate 2. calm, contain, restrain
conceal	*v.*	hide, cover, disguise, mask, camouflage, keep secret
conceit	*n.*	pride, vanity, pomposity
concentrate	*v.*	think carefully, pay attention/regard
concern	*n.*	1. worry, anxiety, bother, upset, distress, interest 2. affair, business, matter, project, enterprise, scheme, plan, venture
concerning	*prep.*	about, of, to do/concerned with
conclude	*v.*	1. end, finish, terminate, complete, close 2. decide, gather, reason, assume

condemn	*v.*	blame, accuse, denounce, convict
condense	*v.*	reduce, contract, shorten, summarize, compress
condition	*n.*	1. state, nature, quality, grade, tone, texture, age 2. provision, stipulation, proviso
conduct	*v.*	1. lead, guide, escort, direct, manage, control 2. carry, convey, transport, transmit
conduct	*n.*	behavior, bearing, carriage
confess	*v.*	admit, own up, declare, acknowledge
confident	*a.*	certain, sure, secure, hopeful, optimistic
confidential	*a.*	not to be disclosed/ revealed/repeated, secret
confine	*v.*	keep in, enclose, contain, cage, imprison, incarcerate
confuse	*v.*	1. mix up, disorder, disarrange, disturb, disarray, jumble, make/cause chaos 2. bewilder, mystify, puzzle, confound, perplex
connect	*v.*	join, unite, fasten, attach, combine, bind, tie, link, couple
conquer	*v.*	beat, defeat, vanquish, overcome, overpower, crush, subdue
consider	*v.*	think about, reflect on, ponder on, heed, pay attention/regard to
considerable	*a.*	large, great, ample, abundant, copious, generous, plentiful
considerate	*a.*	thoughtful, mindful, kind, unselfish, benevolent
construct	*v.*	build, make, erect, put up/together, assemble, compile, compose
consume	*v.*	1. use up, spend, waste/burn away, corrode, rust 2. eat, devour, swallow, drink, imbibe
contain	*v.*	1. hold, comprise, enclose, include 2. calm, restrain, compose
content	*a.*	happy, pleased, glad, satisfied
content	*n.*	filling, constituents, ingredients, capacity, volume
contest	*v.*	dispute, try to disprove, invalidate, argue
contest	*n.*	struggle, combat, battle, competition, dispute, feud, encounter
continue	*v.*	carry/go on, proceed, prolong, extend, add to, keep up
contract	*v.*	1. shorten, condense, reduce, summarize, shrink 2. agree, promise, undertake
contradict	*v.*	deny, gainsay, rebut, refute
control	*v.*	direct, command, regulate, lead, guide, manage, drive
convenient	*a.*	fit, suitable, handy, at hand, available
conversation	*n.*	talk, chat, discussion
cool	*a.*	1. cold, chilly 2. calm, quiet, tranquil, restrained, deliberate, distant
copy	*v.*	imitate, reproduce, duplicate, rewrite, mock, mimic
core	*n.*	center, middle, heart, kernel
correct	*a.*	right, proper, just, exact, accurate
correspond	*v.*	1. agree, match, fit 2. write/send letters, communicate
cost	*n.*	price, value, charge, expense

27

costly	*a.*	expensive, dear, highly-priced, valuable	**credit**	*n.*	reputation, honor, integrity
costume	*n.*	dress, attire, garb, apparel, uniform, suit, robe, outfit		*v.*	believe, accept, acknowledge
council	*n.*	assembly, meeting, gathering, convention	**crew**	*n.*	gang, group, team, band, company
count	*v.*	1. number, reckon, score, calculate, compute	**crime**	*n.*	wrongdoing, offense, sin, misdeed, felony
		2. matter, signify, be significant/important	**crisp**	*a.*	brittle, crusty, snappy
		3. depend, rely, plan	**criticize**	*v.*	find fault, judge, complain
couple	*n.*	pair, two, twosome, duet	**crop**	*n.*	1. harvest, produce, yield
	v.	join, link, tie, connect, unite, bind			2. riding-whip
				v.	trim, cut short, reap
courage	*n.*	bravery, valor, heroism, boldness, fearlessness, pluck	**cross**	*v.*	1. travel across, traverse
course	*n.*	1. route, way, road, path, direction, current			2. oppose, defy
				a.	angry, annoyed, upset
		2. method, technique, plan, progress	**crowd**	*n.*	gathering, group, mass, throng, assembly, mob, multitude
	v.	hunt, chase, pursue	**crude**	*a.*	1. raw, rough, unrefined, natural, native, unpolished
courtesy	*n.*	politeness, good manners, etiquette, civility, respect			2. uncouth, coarse, vulgar, ill-mannered, ungracious
cover	*v.*	conceal, hide, cloak, shield, screen, shelter, enclose, include	**cruel**	*a.*	hurtful, spiteful, unkind, inhuman, inhumane, vindictive, vicious, brutal, savage, barbarous
crack	*v.*	split, fracture, break, splinter	**cruise**	*v.*	sail, voyage
crafty	*a.*	sly, cunning, artful, devious, deceitful, shrewd	**crumble**	*v.*	fall/break into pieces, disintegrate
cram	*v.*	overfill, stuff, jam, ram	**crush**	*v.*	1. crunch, grind, press, squeeze, squash, trample
crash	*n.*	1. loud noise, bang, smash			2. overcome, overpower, subdue, quell, defeat, beat
		2. collision, impact			
		3. failure, ruin	**crust**	*n.*	rind, shell, outer layer, covering
crawl	*v.*	creep, clamber	**cry**	*v.*	1. shout, yell, call out, scream
crazy	*a.*	foolish, silly, absurd, mad, nonsensical, irrational			2. weep, sob, bawl, whine, whimper
create	*v.*	make, devise, design, originate, invent, produce			
creature	*n.*	1. animal, beast	**culprit**	*n.*	offender, guilty person
		2. wretch, unfortunate/ miserable/despicable person			

28

cultivate   *v.*   farm, grow crops, plow, dig, till, improve

cunning   *a.*   sly, crafty, artful, devious, deceitful, shrewd, clever, skillful, ingenious

curb   *v.*   check, control, curtail, bridle, restrict, limit, restrain, hold/keep back

cure   *v.*   heal, make well, relieve, restore, remedy, put right, correct, repair

curious   *a.*   1. inquisitive, prying, searching, inquiring
                       2. interesting, strange, odd, unusual, peculiar, queer

current   *n.*   flow, stream, course
               a.   prevailing, present, common, popular, accepted, widespread

curse   *v.*   1. swear, blaspheme
                       2. wish/bring evil upon, condemn, damn
              n.   suffering, bane

curve   *n.*   bend, turn, curvature, arch, arc

custom   *n.*   habit, rule, fashion, practice, manner, tradition

customer   *n.*   buyer, purchaser, client

cut   *v.*   1. divide, sever, wound, gash, slash, slit, puncture, clip, snip
                       2. ignore, cold-shoulder, boycott

D d

dabble   *v.*   1. wet, moisten, splash
2. have a go, try out, meddle, participate, take part

daily   *adv.*   every day, each day, often, frequently
       n.   newspaper, journal

dainty   *a.*   1. neat, nice, delicate, pleasing, choice, tasteful, refined, exquisite
2. clean, particular, fastidious

damage   *v.*   injure, hurt, harm, afflict, disfigure, break, abuse, sabotage

damp   *v.*   1. dampen, moisten, make humid
2. discourage
Her indifference **damped** his ardor.

danger   *n.*   risk, peril, threat, menace, hazard, jeopardy

dare   *v.*   1. attempt, venture
2. challenge, defy

daring   *a.*   bold, brave, valiant, venturesome, adventurous, fearless, courageous, undaunted

dark   *a.*   without light/illumination, unlit, sunless, dim, dull, somber, gloomy, murky, indistinct, obscure, drab, dreary, cheerless

darling   *n.*   sweetheart, dearest, pet, favorite, loved one, beloved

dart   *v.*   fly, spring, run, rush, dash, race, spurt
       n.   arrow, missile, javelin

dash   *v.*   1. run quickly/swiftly/speedily/fast/rapidly, race, sprint, spurt
2. smash/crash/bang on/against
3. discourage, spoil, frustrate

dawn   *n.*   1. daybreak, break of day, sunrise
2. beginning, start, commencement, origin
dawn on: *grow/become clear/plain to*

day   *n.*   1. daylight, daytime
2. 24 hours

daydream   *v.*   fancy, imagine, build castles in the air, have pipe-dreams, fantasize

daze   *v.*   bewilder, confuse, mix up, stun

dazzle   *v.*   blind, confuse
       n.   glare, blinding light

dead   *a.*   numb, insensitive, dull, lifeless, not living/alive, deceased, extinct

deaden   *v.*   numb, dull, diminish, soften, lessen, soothe, alleviate, cushion, muffle, smother

deadly   *a.*   fatal, mortal, lethal, destructive, poisonous, harmful

deaf   *a.*   1. unable to hear
2. unwilling to hear/listen, heedless, inattentive, unmindful

deal   *v.*   1. handle, manage
2. trade, do business
3. deliver, distribute, give/hand out

dealer   *n.*   trader, merchant, distributor, wholesaler, shopkeeper, retailer

dear   *a.*   1. dearest, darling, beloved, cherished, favorite
2. not cheap, costly, expensive

debate	*v.*	argue, discuss, dispute, contest, wrangle
debt	*n.*	debit, money/property owed/owing, due, duty, obligation
decay	*v.*	rot, wither, fade, waste away, deteriorate, putrefy, decompose, spoil, rust, corrode
deceive	*v.*	cheat, swindle, hoax, mislead, trick, fool, bluff, dissemble
decent	*a.*	proper, respectable, becoming, seemly, modest, not vulgar/rude/obscene
decide	*v.*	settle, fix, arrange, rule, resolve, determine, conclude
declare	*v.*	state, announce, proclaim, admit, reveal, assert
decline	*v.*	1. refuse, reject, not accept 2. drop, lessen, reduce, depreciate, decrease, diminish, fall lower, weaken, become feeble/frail/infirm
decorate	*v.*	beautify, adorn
decrease	*v.*	lessen, reduce, diminish, lower, shrink, contract, drop, fall, decline, depreciate, soften
deed	*n.*	act, action, feat, performance
defeat	*v.*	beat, overcome, overpower, subdue, conquer, vanquish, quell, rout
	n.	failure, loss
defect	*n.*	fault, flaw, blemish, imperfection
	v.	desert, run away
defend	*v.*	protect, maintain, guard, shield, support
definite	*a.*	exact, fixed, accurate, precise, certain, sure, clear, distinct, decided
deformed	*a.*	misshapen, malformed, warped, twisted, distorted, disfigured, crippled, lame
defraud	*v.*	cheat, swindle, rob, deceive, trick
defy	*v.*	1. dare, challenge, resist, oppose, mock 2. disregard, ignore, flout
delay	*v.*	1. postpone, put back, retard, hinder 2. linger, loiter, dawdle, hang about, hesitate, wait
deliberate	*a.*	intentional, fully considered
deliberate	*v.*	consider, think over/about
delicacy	*n.*	1. weakness, feebleness, tenderness, daintiness, fineness, diplomacy 2. fine/dainty/tasty food
delicate	*a.*	1. fine, dainty, tender, fragile 2. feeble, weak, frail, infirm
delicious	*a.*	tasty, sweet, luscious, dainty, enjoyable, pleasing
delight	*v.*	please, charm, thrill, make happy/glad/joyful, enchant, entrance, amuse, entertain
deliver	*v.*	1. hand over, transfer, bring, distribute 2. set free, liberate, rescue, save
demand	*v.*	ask, claim, request, apply, urge
demolish	*v.*	destroy, put down, wreck, ruin, smash, raze
den	*n.*	nest, lair, retreat, cave
dense	*a.*	1. thick, concentrated, compact, solid, close, lush 2. stupid, slow-minded
deny	*v.*	1. contradict, gainsay, dispute, disprove, refute 2. refuse, withhold

depart	*v.*	leave, go, go away, go/start out, withdraw, quit
depend	*v.*	rely, trust/be confident in
depression	*n.*	1. hollow, dent, cavity, indentation 2. sadness, misery, unhappiness, gloominess, dejection
deputy	*n.*	substitute, assistant, agent, representative, delegate
derelict	*a.*	forsaken, abandoned, vacated, deserted, neglected
descend	*v.*	go/get down, drop, fall, sink, settle, dismount, alight
descent	*n.*	fall, drop, slope, incline, declivity
describe	*v.*	write/speak/talk about, explain, report on, outline, express
desert	*v.*	forsake, abandon, leave, vacate, neglect
desert	*a.* *n.*	barren, empty, infertile barren/empty/infertile land
deserted	*a.*	empty, vacant, forsaken, abandoned
deserve	*v.*	earn, merit, win, rate, be worthy of
design	*n.*	1. pattern, decoration, plan, sketch, drawing 2. intention, object, aim, scheme, idea, notion, creation
desirable	*a.*	wanted, desired, worthy, worthwhile, acceptable, good
desire	*v.*	want, wish/crave/yearn for
desolate	*a.*	1. lone, alone, forlorn, unhappy, sad, wretched, miserable 2. lonely, deserted
despair	*n.*	discouragement, hopelessness, pessimism
desperate	*a.*	1. rash, reckless, bold, wild, savage, ferocious, careless 2. hopeless, unpromising
despise	*v.*	scorn, treat with contempt, dislike, disapprove of
destroy	*v.*	pull/knock down, demolish, end, finish, wreck, ruin, smash, raze, annihilate
detach	*v.*	take/pull off, remove, disconnect, loosen, unfasten, separate
detain	*v.*	hold, arrest, keep waiting, retard, delay, hinder
detect	*v.*	find, discover, notice, see, perceive, observe
detective	*n.*	investigator, sleuth
determine	*v.*	decide, resolve, arrange, assess, estimate, find out, learn
determined	*a.*	firm, adamant, resolved, resolute, stubborn, obdurate, obstinate
detest	*v.*	hate, dislike intensely, abhor, loathe
develop	*v.*	improve slowly/gradually, expand, enlarge, increase, extend
device	*n.*	1. gadget, contrivance, invention, apparatus, trick, scheme, plan, arrangement
devoted	*a.*	loyal, faithful, true, constant, dedicated, earnest, sincere
devour	*v.*	consume, eat up greedily/voraciously, swallow
dictate	*v.*	1. give orders/instructions/commands/directions 2. say, tell
die	*v.*	expire, depart, fade/pass away, wither, decline, perish

different	*a.*	dissimilar, unusual, uncommon, special, novel, unalike, not alike
difficulty	*n.*	problem, snag, obstacle, dilemma, complication, bother, trouble, burden, hardship, plight, predicament
dignity	*n.*	eminence, worthiness, pride, grandeur, majesty, nobility, stateliness
diligent	*a.*	industrious, hard-working, constant, steady, assiduous
dim	*a.*	dull, faint, indistinct, obscure, vague, dark, cloudy, inconspicuous
din	*n.*	row, noise, uproar, babble, clamor, tumult, racket, bedlam, pandemonium
dingy	*a.*	shabby, faded, grimy, dirty, squalid
dip	*n.*	1. immersion, dive 2. swim, bathe 3. hollow, downwards slope
direct	*a.*	1. straight, express, short 2. outspoken
	v.	1. govern, control, order, command, manage 2. address, send, aim, conduct
direction	*n.*	1. way, course, aim, route, path 2. order, instruction, rule, regulation
directly	*adv.*	at once, immediately, now
dirt	*n.*	muck, mud, soil, soot, filth, impurity, pollution, contamination, squalor
disaster	*n.*	catastrophe, tragedy, calamity, great misfortune
discipline	*n.*	obedience, order, instruction, training, control, self-control
discuss	*v.*	debate, talk over
disgrace	*v.*	put to shame, dishonor, disfavor, defame, degrade
disguise	*v.*	hide, conceal, mask, camouflage, veil
disgusting	*a.*	revolting, repulsive, loathsome, nasty, disgraceful
dismal	*a.*	dreary, drab, not cheerful, cheerless, dingy, sad, miserable, doleful, gloomy, mournful, lugubrious
dismiss	*v.*	send away/off, discharge
displace	*v.*	take/change the place of, remove, move, shift, disarrange
display	*n.*	show, exhibition, parade, presentation, demonstration
	v.	show, exhibit, parade, demonstrate
displease	*v.*	offend, annoy, vex, make indignant
distant	*a.*	1. far away/off, remote, at a distance 2. cold, frigid, indifferent, shy, reticent, reserved
distinct	*a.*	1. clear, plain, definite, obvious 2. separate, different, unconnected
distress	*n.*	trouble, grief, worry, concern, anxiety, unhappiness, sadness, misery, discomfort, pain
distribute	*v.*	hand/give out, deal, share, broadcast, scatter, sow
distrust	*n.*	doubt, disbelief, suspicion
disturb	*v.*	bother, worry, pester, molest, agitate, annoy, irritate, upset
divide	*v.*	separate, cut, break up, part, distribute, share
do	*v.*	make, act, accomplish, perform, achieve
dodge	*v.*	avoid, evade, move aside, duck, side-step
	n.	device, trick, scheme, plan

33

donate	*v.*	give, contribute, present
doubtful	*a.*	uncertain, unsure, suspicious, distrustful, dubious, undecided, wavering, indefinite
doubtless	*adv.*	without a/any doubt, certainly, surely, decidedly, definitely
drab	*a.*	dull, dreary, shabby, monotonous, tedious, gloomy, plain
drag	*v.*	pull, haul, tow, tug, draw
drain	*v.*	empty, flow
	n.	waste-pipe, gutter, outlet, trench, conduit, channel
drastic	*a.*	violent, vigorous, ruthless
draw	*v.*	1. attract, pull, haul, drag, tow, tug
		2. sketch, design
dreadful	*a.*	fearful, alarming, terrible, awful, horrible, atrocious, dire
dream	*n.*	fancy, vision, trance, nightmare
dreary	*a.*	drab, dull, tedious, bleak, barren, cheerless, dismal, dingy, gloomy
dress	*n.*	clothes, clothing, garments, attire, apparel, garb, costume, robes
drift	*v.*	wander, float
drill	*v.*	1. exercise
		2. bore
drive	*v.*	1. guide, control, direct, steer, pilot
		2. urge, press, persuade, compel, make, prod

drop	*n.*	1. fall, descent, dive
		2. tiny amount/quantity, ball, globule
		3. sip, taste
drown	*v.*	1. flood, drench, soak
		2. stifle, suffocate, extinguish, muffle, deaden
drowsy	*a.*	sleepy, sluggish, lethargic, languid
dry	*a.*	1. without water/moisture, waterless, arid
		2. thirsty, parched
		3. dull, boring, tedious, uninteresting, dreary
dual	*a.*	twofold, double
due	*a.*	1. owing, unpaid, payable
		2. expected, awaited
		3. rightful, suitable, appropriate
dull	*a.*	1. dim, not bright, faint, obscure, indistinct, cloudy, sunless
		2. blunt
		3. stupid, dense, backward
duplicate	*v.*	copy, imitate, repeat, reproduce
duty	*n.*	1. obligation, service, office, function, engagement
		2. tax, payment, demand
dwell	*v.*	live, reside, abide, lodge, inhabit
dwindle	*v.*	lessen, reduce, diminish, decrease, shrink, fade away
dye	*n.*	paint, pigment, coloring matter, stain

E e

each   *a.*   every
         pron. each/everyone

eager   *a.*   keen, enthusiastic, earnest, zealous, greatly desirous, willing, determined, passionate, ardent, fervent

early   *adv.*   beforehand, before time, in advance
       a.   long ago, of bygone days/times/ages, former

earn   *v.*   gain, obtain, acquire, get, achieve, attain, work for, be rewarded with, deserve, merit, rate

earnest   *a.*   determined, serious, keen, zealous, willing, enthusiastic, passionate, ardent, eager, sincere, honest, true

ease   *n.*   rest, relaxation, calm, comfort, leisure, quiet, easiness, simplicity
       v.   reduce, lessen, minimize, relieve, soothe, alleviate, palliate

easy   *a.*   restful, relaxed, calm, comfortable, leisurely, without effort, effortless not hard/difficult, simple, facile, fluent

eat   *v.*   1. dine, consume, feed/feast on, devour
           2. wear away, corrode, rust, erode

eccentric   *a.*   1. odd, strange, queer, peculiar, unusual, uncommon, bizarre, irregular, whimsical
           2. not concentric/circular

edge   *n.*   margin, boundary, border, verge, rim, brink
       v.   1. sharpen
           2. make/furnish a border to/for .
           3. move slowly/little by little, insinuate

edible   *a.*   eatable, wholesome, nutritious

educate   *v.*   teach, instruct, train, tutor, enlighten, inform, guide, lead, bring up (children)

effect   *n.*   result, outcome, consequence, impression
       v.   do, complete, put into effect, expedite, accomplish

effective   *a.*   1. able, capable; competent, efficient, actual, existing
           2. striking, pleasing, attractive

efficient   *a.*   able, capable, competent, effective, skillful, well-organized, well-managed, business-like

effort   *n.*   1. attempt, try, endeavor, essay, application
           2. work, labor, toil, industry, exertion, energy, action, activity

elaborate   *a.*   decorative, ornamental, elegant, ornate, overdone

elaborate   *v.*   explain, specify, exaggerate, embroider, expand, extend

elapse   *v.*   go/pass by/away

elastic   *a.*   springy, stretchy, pliable, flexible, resilient, supple

elated   *a.*   excited, merry, gleeful, joyful, overjoyed, carried away, overcome

elect   *v.*   choose, select, pick
       n.   best, most worthy/deserving, privileged

elegant   *a.*   graceful, beautiful, handsome, stylish, tasteful, refined, excellent, accomplished

elementary	*a.*	simple, easy, basic, fundamental, introductory, rudimentary
eliminate	*v.*	leave out, remove, erase, abolish, expel, discharge
eloquent	*a.*	well-spoken, fluent, rhetorical
embark	*v.*	board, go aboard/on board, set out, depart
embarrass	*v.*	make uncomfortable, discomfort, confuse, disconcert, bewilder, perplex, encumber, impede, complicate
emblem	*n.*	badge, mark, symbol, sign, token, device, crest
embrace	*v.*	1. hug, clasp, cuddle, hold 2. include, contain, comprise, accept eagerly
emerge	*v.*	come into view, appear, arise
emergency	*n.*	urgent/desperate situation, crisis, dilemma
eminent	*a.*	famous, celebrated, renowned, notable, noted, illustrious, exalted
emphasize	*v.*	stress, accent, accentuate, bring into prominence
employ	*v.*	use, give work to, find work for, engage, hire, appoint, retain
empty	*v.*	void, evacuate, pour out, drain, exhaust
	a.	vacant, unoccupied, deserted, bare, desolate, hollow, bereft
encamp	*v.*	erect/pitch tents, make/form a camp
enchant	*v.*	charm, delight, please, captivate, beguile, entrance, bewitch
enclose	*v.*	contain, surround, encircle, envelop, enfold, wrap, conceal, hide

encounter	*v.*	meet, come across, bump into
encourage	*v.*	stimulate, embolden, give support to, inspire, hearten, cheer, invite
end	*v.*	finish, terminate, cease, stop, conclude, finalize
	n.	1. aim, object, intention, result 2. tip, point, extremity
endanger	*v.*	put/place in danger/jeopardy/peril, imperil
endless	*a.*	boundless, limitless, everlasting, continual, continuous, ceaseless, incessant, uninterrupted, perpetual, eternal, forever
endure	*v.*	1. put up with, bear, suffer, tolerate, submit to, undergo 2. last, exist, live, continue, remain
enemy	*n.*	foe, adversary, antagonist, opponent
energetic	*a.*	active, vigorous, lusty, brisk, lively, alive, zestful, enthusiastic, zealous
energy	*n.*	vigor, power, force, enthusiasm, keenness, zeal, zest, stamina
enfold	*v.*	enclose, wrap, clasp, embrace, encircle, envelop, surround, conceal, hide, contain
engage	*v.*	1. employ, hire, find work for, appoint 2. undertake, promise, guarantee, contract 3. begin to fight/grapple, encounter, attack
engulf	*v.*	swallow up, envelop, overwhelm
enjoyment	*n.*	pleasure, delight, joy, happiness, gladness, amusement

36

enlarge	*v.*	make larger/bigger/wider, increase, expand, magnify, extend
enlighten	*v.*	1. give light to, brighten, illuminate
		2. teach, instruct, educate, inform, advise
enormous	*a.*	giant, gigantic, huge, tremendous, vast, immense, monstrous
enough	*a.*	ample, adequate, sufficient
enquire	*v.*	*see* **inquire**
enrage	*v.*	anger, vex, annoy, make furious, infuriate, madden, aggravate
ensure	*v.*	make sure/certain/safe
enter	*v.*	1. go/come into, invade
		2. make an entry, register, record
enterprise	*n.*	venture, project, plan, scheme, undertaking, task
entertain	*v.*	amuse, delight, divert, beguile
enthusiasm	*n.*	keenness, eagerness, zeal, zest, willingness, determination, passion
entice	*v.*	tempt, lure, attract, bait, coax, persuade, induce
entire	*a.*	complete, whole, full, total
entrance	*n.*	entry, way in, opening, approach, access, doorway, gateway
entrance	*v.*	charm, delight, beguile, captivate, enchant, bewitch
environment	*n.*	surroundings, habitat, neighborhood
envy	*n.*	jealousy, desire, covetousness
episode	*n.*	incident, event, occasion, happening, occurrence
equal	*a.*	alike, the same, equivalent, identical, even, uniform
equip	*v.*	supply, provide, furnish, fit out
equivalent	*a.*	alike, the same, equal
erase	*v.*	eradicate, rub out, efface, remove
erect	*v.*	build, construct, assemble, put up, raise
	a.	upright, perpendicular, vertical
err	*v.*	make a mistake/error, do wrong, blunder, default, sin
errand	*n.*	mission, expedition, journey, purpose/object of journey
error	*n.*	mistake, fault, blunder, wrong
erupt	*v.*	burst out, explode, blow up, discharge
escape	*v.*	1 become free, be free/released/liberated, leak, depart, take flight, flee, make off, steal away
		2. avoid, evade, elude, dodge
escort	*v.*	protect, guard, accompany, guide, lead, conduct
essential	*a.*	necessary, needful, needed, requisite, vital, fundamental, very important
establish	*v.*	1. found, build, institute, set up
		2. prove, confirm
estimate	*v.*	assess, calculate, judge, gauge, measure
eternal	*a.*	everlasting, for ever, continual, continuous, ceaseless, incessant, perpetual, endless, abiding
evade	*v.*	avoid, dodge, escape, elude
evaporate	*v.*	1. vaporize, become a vapor
		2. vanish, disappear, become invisible, dissolve

even	*a.*	level, flat, smooth, regular, not odd, uniform, exact, exactly divisible by two
event	*n.*	incident, happening, occurrence, episode, affair, occasion
eventually	*adv.*	at last, in time, lastly, finally, ultimately
everlasting	*a.*	eternal, perpetual, for ever, continuous, continual, ceaseless, incessant, endless, abiding
evident	*a.*	plain, clear, true, obvious, apparent
evil	*n.*	wickedness, sinfulness, wrongdoing, malevolence, vice, immorality, sin, harm
exact	*a.*	correct, precise, just, true, definite, accurate
	v.	demand, insist on
exaggerate	*v.*	magnify, overstate, romanticize, elaborate, embroider, stretch, enlarge, expand, amplify
examine	*v.*	check, test, inspect, observe, look at, search, investigate
example	*n.*	specimen, model, pattern, sample, illustration
exasperate	*v.*	vex, provoke, irritate, aggravate, annoy
exceed	*v.*	be more/larger/greater than, surpass, go beyond
excel	*v.*	be better than/superior to, do well, surpass, beat
excellent	*a.*	exceptional, outstanding, superior, perfect, superb, admirable
exceptional	*a.*	outstanding, special, rare, unusual, uncommon, extraordinary
excess	*n.*	1. surplus, abundance 2. outrage, intemperance

excite	*v.*	arouse, enliven, stir, agitate, disturb, stimulate, provoke
exclaim	*v.*	cry/call out, shout
exclude	*v.*	leave/shut out, omit, disregard, reject, expel, oust, banish
excursion	*n.*	trip, outing, journey, expedition, tour
excuse	*v.*	pardon, overlook, condone, forgive
	n.	apology, explanation, plea, defense
execute	*v.*	1. do, carry out, perform, expedite, effect 2. put to death, kill, liquidate
exercise	*n.*	task, activity, drill, maneuver
exertion	*n.*	effort, endeavor, toil, work, labor, industry
exhaust	*v.*	1. tire, weary, fatigue, weaken, enfeeble 2. use up, consume, empty, drain
exhibit	*v.*	display, show, present, reveal, expose
exist	*v.*	live, survive
exit	*n.*	way out, outlet, withdrawal, departure
expand	*v.*	increase, enlarge, magnify, amplify, swell, distend, dilate, extend, stretch, spread
expect	*v.*	await, anticipate, hope for, look forward to
expel	*v.*	turn/drive/throw out, eject, banish, exile, oust, send/chase away, exclude
expense	*n.*	cost, charge, amount, total, sum, outlay
expensive	*a.*	not cheap, costly, dear, high-priced

experience	*v.*	undergo, encounter, endure, suffer
	n.	1. happening, occurrence, event
		2. ordeal, trial
		3. practice, training
expert	*a.*	skillful, adept, proficient, talented, clever, well-qualified, well-trained
explain	*v.*	clarify, elucidate, elaborate, demonstrate, show
exploit	*v.*	take advantage of, gain/profit/benefit from, use
	n.	brave/striking act/action/deed, venture, adventure, escapade, feat, stunt, achievement
explore	*v.*	search, examine, look at, inspect, survey, reconnoiter
expose	*v.*	1. uncover, bare, disclose, show, exhibit
		2. discredit
express	*a.*	quick, fast, rapid, speedy, swift, without delay/interruptions, unretarded
	v.	state, declare, assert, indicate
expression	*n.*	1. statement, remark, declaration, explanation
		2. look, show, appearance
exquisite	*a.*	keen, acute, fine, delicate, dainty, lovely, choice, superb
extend	*v.*	1. stretch, elongate, lengthen, expand, enlarge, increase, spread
		2. offer, give
extent	*n.*	size, amount, quantity, expanse, scope
exterior	*a.*	outside, outer, outward, external
exterminate	*v.*	destroy, liquidate, abolish, wipe out, kill
external	*a.*	exterior, outside, outward, outer
extra	*a.*	additional, supplementary, surplus, spare
extract	*n.*	quotation, passage (from a book), section, part, portion, essence
	v.	pull/draw/take out, remove, withdraw
extraordinary	*a.*	strange, uncommon, unusual, rare, out of the ordinary, incredible, amazing, astounding, remarkable, astonishing
extravagance	*n.*	reckless/foolish/needless waste, excess, lavishness, liberality
extreme	*a.*	farthest, utmost, most distant/remote
extremely	*adv.*	exceedingly, outstandingly, exceptionally
eye	*v.*	look at, regard, view, observe, watch carefully
		eye-opener: *surprise, shock, revelation*

F f

fable	*n.*	story, tale, legend, myth
fabricate	*v.*	1. make, manufacture, construct 2. lie, be untruthful, invent
fabulous	*a.*	legendary, mythical, fictitious, unreal, fanciful, incredible, astonishing, wonderful, extraordinary
face	*n.*	1. visage, countenance 2. front, outside, exterior
	v.	meet, encounter, confront, oppose, defy
fade	*v.*	grow/become dim/faint, lose color, wither, droop, wane
fail	*v.*	1. miss, neglect, omit, be unsuccessful 2. disappoint, let down 3. weaken, become feeble, decline, deteriorate
faint	*v.*	swoon, droop, falter, weaken
	a.	1. weak, feeble, languid 2. not clear/distinct, unclear, indistinct, dim, vague, faded
fair	*a.*	1. just, right, correct, proper, impartial, honest 2. fine, handsome, pleasing, attractive, beautiful 3. bright, clear, fine, sunny 4. average, passable, acceptable
	n.	market, wake
faith	*n.*	belief, trust, confidence, devotion, loyalty, religion
faithful	*a.*	loyal, true, constant, sure, devoted, reliable, dependable, trustworthy, resolute
fake	*a.*	sham, bogus, fraudulent, counterfeit, forged, false, imitation, not authentic
fall	*v.*	1. drop, descend, plunge, tumble, topple, go down 2. lower, lessen, diminish, decline, depreciate
false	*a.*	1. sham, imitation, bogus, fake, counterfeit, forged, artificial, fraudulent, not authentic, make-believe, pretentious 2. not true/correct, untrue, incorrect, wrong, mistaken, erroneous 3. disloyal, unfaithful, inconstant, treacherous, not trustworthy
fame	*n.*	renown, reputation, prestige
familiar	*a.*	1. well-known, common, commonplace, ordinary, everyday 2. friendly, informal, sociable, companionable, intimate
family	*n.*	kith, kin, kindred, folk, tribe, relations, relatives, household
famine	*n.*	hunger, starvation, dearth/shortage of food
famous	*a.*	famed, celebrated, great, notable, noted, well-known, illustrious, renowned
fancy	*n.*	idea, notion, belief, supposition, conjecture, whim, fantasy, imagination
	a.	decorated, ornamental, ornate, pretty, gaudy
fantastic	*a.*	fanciful, imagined, whimsical, absurd, weird, strange, peculiar, farfetched, fabulous, wonderful
far	*a.*	distant, remote **farfetched:** *exaggerated, embroidered, romanticized, unbelievable*

fare   *v.*   1. live, exist, manage, turn out, be fed/accommodated/entertained
           2. go, travel, journey
           fare forth: *set/start out*
      n.   1. fee, charge, payment (for a journey)
           2. food, eatables, victuals, provisions

farewell   *n.*   good-bye, adieu, leave-taking, parting

farm   *v.*   cultivate, till
      n.   farmstead, holding

farther   *a.*   more distant/remote/extended

fascinate   *v.*   charm, entrance, enchant, attract, entice

fashion   *v.*   make, shape, mold, form, design, create, invent
      n.   style, mode, vogue, custom, tradition, manner, way

fast   *a.*   1. quick, rapid, swift, speedy, fleet, lively, nimble, brisk, vigorous
           2. secure, stable, fixed, firm, tight
      v.   hunger, starve, go without food

fasten   *v.*   secure, fix, attach, tie, knot, bind, join, connect, couple, link, anchor

fat   *n.*   grease, oil
      a.   plump, stout, gross, corpulent, obese, well-fed

fatal   *a.*   deadly, ruinous, mortal, lethal

fate   *n.*   fortune, luck, lot, destiny, doom

fatigue   *v.*   tire out, weary, exhaust, enfeeble, weaken

fault   *n.*   1. defect, flaw, imperfection, weakness, failing, disadvantage, mistake, error
           2. wrong, offense, sin

favor   *v.*   befriend, be kind to, prefer

favorable   *a.*   friendly, helpful, kind, kindly, beneficial, useful, promising, hopeful, well-disposed, propitious

fear   *n.*   dread, terror, fright, horror, dismay, apprehension, alarm

fearless   *a.*   bold, brave, courageous, gallant, undaunted, dauntless, valiant, daring, heroic

feast   *n.*   meal, banquet, festival, fête, holiday, anniversary

feat   *n.*   deed, exploit, achievement, accomplishment, attainment

feature   *n.*   outstanding part, characteristic quality

feeble   *a.*   weak, slight, puny, delicate, frail, exhausted, languid, listless

feel   *v.*   1. touch, contact, handle, grope
           2. be moved/affected/touched

feeling   *n.*   touch, sense of touch, sensation, emotion, thought

feminine   *a.*   female, womanly, ladylike, soft, tender, gentle

fence   *n.*   boundary, bar, barrier, rail, railing, barricade, hedge
      v.   1. enclose, encircle, engage
           2. evade, prevaricate

ferocious   *a.*   fierce, savage, wild, untamed, brutal, bestial, barbarous, cruel

fertile   *a.*   not barren, viable, rich, productive, fruitful, cultivated, fecund

fetch   *n.*   bring, carry, transport, obtain, get

feud   *n.*   perpetual quarrel/battle/hostility/dispute

41

fever	*n.*	1. eagerness, excitement, passion 2. illness, sickness, disease
fidget	*v.*	fret, fuss, be restless/ill at ease, toss, turn
field	*n.*	1. land, area, range 2. battlefield, battleground, sportsground
fierce	*a.*	ferocious, savage, wild, furious, fiery
fight	*n.*	struggle, combat, battle, action, contest, fray, encounter
figure	*n.*	1. shape, outline, form, pattern, body, image 2. digit, number
fill	*v.*	become full, pack, store, stuff, pour/put in, satiate
final	*a.*	end, last, terminal, concluding
finale	*n.*	end, finish, conclusion
find	*v.*	discover, detect, recover, search/look for
fine	*a.*	1. very thin, delicate, of good quality 2. handsome, choice, excellent 3. dry, clear, sunny, bright
	n.	penalty, forfeit
finish	*v.*	end, finalize, terminate, conclude, complete, close
firm	*a.*	fixed, stable, steady, sturdy, solid, hard, tight, secure, steadfast, determined, resolute, adamant
fit	*v.*	agree, suit, match, be right/proper/appropriate/apt/suitable
	n.	seizure, spasm, bout, whim, notion
fix	*v.*	1. fasten, join, attach, secure 2. mend, repair, adjust 3. decide, arrange, settle, determine
	n.	problem, difficulty, predicament

flabby	*a.*	limp, slack, soft, loose, flaccid, fleshy, fat
flake	*n.*	scale, shaving, tuft
flame	*v.*	1. blaze, flare, burn, be on fire 2. be eager/enthusiastic/zealous/passionate 3. be angry/annoyed/in a temper
flash	*n.*	1. gleam, glow, light, flare, sparkle 2. instant, moment, second
flat	*a.*	1. level, horizontal, even, smooth 2. tasteless, stale, dull, insipid
flavor	*n.*	taste, relish, piquancy
	v.	season, salt, add herbs/spices/condiments, spice
flaw	*n.*	defect, imperfection, fault, weakness
flawless	*a.*	without defects, perfect
flee	*v.*	run away, escape, depart hurriedly, fly
flexible	*a.*	springy, elastic, stretchy, supple, pliant, pliable, resilient
flicker	*v.*	flutter, waver, quiver, quaver, shake, twitch, fluctuate, shimmer, flare, flash
flight	*n.*	1. escape, rapid departure 2. air transport, journey by air/airplane, trajectory, glide **flight of steps:** *stairs, stairway, staircase*
fling	*v.*	hurl, throw, cast, toss, project, heave, pitch
float	*v.*	drift, hover, sail, be afloat/buoyant
flock	*n.*	group, herd, gathering, congregation, assembly, crowd, company, throng, followers, adherents

flourish	*v.*	1. do well, thrive, succeed, prosper 2. brandish, wave about
flow	*v.*	pour out, stream, course, gush, flood, run, glide
fluster	*v.*	upset, confuse, flurry, flutter, bustle, fuss, bother, agitate
fly	*v.*	1. flee, escape, run away 2. be in flight, take/make an air journey, soar, wing, glide
foe	*n.*	enemy, adversary, opponent, antagonist, rival
foggy	*a.*	misty, cloudy, murky, blurred, hazy, nebulous, vague, dim, unsure, unclear, obscure
folk	*n.*	people, persons, kin, kith, kindred, kinfolk, relations, relatives, tribe, race
follow	*v.*	1. pursue, hunt, chase, run/come/go after, track, trace 2. copy, imitate 3. support, adhere to, observe 4. understand, comprehend
fond	*a.*	affectionate, loving, caring, devoted, doting, tender, kind
food	*n.*	nutriment, nourishment, fare, victuals, eatables, rations
fool	*n.*	idiot, clown, buffoon, oaf, silly person, simpleton, nitwit, dunce
	v.	1. jest, joke, play, clown 2. deceive, hoodwink, dupe, trick, outwit, mislead
foolhardy	*a.*	reckless, rash, risky, headstrong, impetuous, thoughtless, foolish
foot	*n.*	bottom, base
forbid	*v.*	disallow, prohibit, ban, prevent
forbidding	*a.*	threatening, frightening, menacing, unpleasant, baleful
force	*v.*	make, compel, drive, induce, oblige
	n.	strength, power, might, energy, effort
forecast	*v.*	foresee, foretell, predict, prophesy, presage, portend
foreign	*a.*	1. alien, from abroad/another country 2. strange, unknown, unfamiliar, unaccustomed
forget	*v.*	fail to remember/recall/recollect, overlook
forgive	*v.*	pardon, excuse, let off, overlook
forlorn	*a.*	without friends, lonely, friendless, forsaken, deserted, neglected, dejected, woebegone, downcast, unhappy, sad, miserable, woeful
form	*n.*	shape, outline, figure, body, pattern, plan, design, formation
former	*a.*	earlier, preceding, previous, foregoing, prior
forsake	*v.*	desert, abandon, leave, neglect, quit, depart from, vacate, give up, disown, abdicate
fortunate	*a.*	lucky, favored, prosperous, successful
fortune	*n.*	1. luck, fate, chance, lot, destiny 2. wealth, prosperity, riches, success
foul	*a.*	1. unfair, distasteful, vulgar, nasty, unpleasant, reprehensible 2. dirty, tainted, blemished, sullied, decayed, filthy, putrefied, unclean, polluted

foundation	*n.*	1. bottom, base, groundwork, footing, foot, support 2. institution, establishment, organization
fraction	*n.*	part, portion, piece, bit, section, division
fracture	*v.*	break, snap, rupture, split, crack
fragile	*a.*	easily broken/damaged, breakable, flimsy, weak, delicate, brittle, frail
fragment	*n.*	small piece/part/fraction, bit, morsel, scrap, chip, splinter
fragrance	*n.*	perfume, scent, pleasant odor/smell
frantic	*a.*	desperate, fearful, very agitated, panicky, panicking, frenzied, excited, crazy
free	*a.*	1. liberated, at liberty, loose, independent, released, discharged, unfastened 2. open, frank, candid 3. liberal, generous, open-handed, lavish 4. at no charge, gratis
frequent	*a.*	repeated, numerous, regular, many
frequent	*v.*	visit often/many times, haunt
fresh	*a.*	1. new, recent, novel, different, refreshing 2. brisk, lively, invigorating, bracing, vigorous, healthy 3. inexperienced, green, raw, gullible
fret	*v.*	1. worry, be concerned/agitated, fuss, vex, annoy, irritate 2. wear away, erode, corrode
friendly	*a.*	affectionate, agreeable, sociable, companionable, neighborly, kind, helpful

frighten	*v.*	make afraid/fearful, terrify, scare, alarm, intimidate
frightful	*a.*	dreadful, terrible, shocking, awful, fearful, horrid, horrible, ghastly
front	*n.*	face, foremost part, outside, exterior
	v.	face, confront, encounter, oppose, defy
frown	*v.*	scowl, look sour/sullen **frown upon:** *disapprove of*
fruitful	*a.*	fertile, productive, gainful, profitable, rich, abundant
frustrate	*v.*	thwart, oppose, defeat
fugitive	*n.*	runaway, escapee
fulfill	*v.*	carry out, accomplish, achieve, complete, finish, end
full	*a.*	1. complete, comprehensive, whole, total, entire 2. filled, occupied with
fun	*n.*	amusement, entertainment, merriment, gaiety, glee, jollity, mirth, frolic, sport, play
funny	*a.*	1. amusing, comical, humorous, mirthful, laughable 2. peculiar, odd, strange, queer, unusual
furious	*a.*	angry, raging, enraged, irate, infuriated, wild, mad, maddened, flaming, frenzied, violent, fierce, wrathful
furnish	*v.*	provide, give, equip, supply, outfit
further	*a.*	additional, more distant
furthermore	*adv.*	moreover, what is more, besides, also, additionally
fury	*n.*	rage, frenzy, anger, ire, wrath, ferocity
fuss	*v.*	bother, worry, fidget, fret
futile	*a.*	vain, pointless, empty, worthless, unprofitable, unsuccessful

G g

gabble   *v.*   jabber, gibber, prattle, gab, babble, chatter, speak unintelligibly/excessively/confusedly, be incoherent/inarticulate, talk foolishly/idly/wildly

gadget   *n.*   device, contrivance, small fitting

gag   *v.*   1. silence with a gag
              2. choke, retch, strangle
       n.   joke, trick, comedy situation

gain   *v.*   obtain, get, acquire, receive, win, come to own/possess, collect, glean, achieve, attain, procure

gallant   *a.*   brave, bold, daring, dashing, courageous, unafraid, fearless, valiant, valorous, dauntless, undaunted, heroic

gallery   *n.*   long corridor/hall, portico, colonnade, platform, theater balcony, room for an art exhibition

gamble   *v.*   bet, wager, back, take risks

game   *n.*   1. sport, play, amusement, fun, athletic contest, match
              2. scheme, undertaking, plan, project, dodge, trick
              3. quarry, wild animal (hunted for food), prey
       a.   1. brave, bold, daring, plucky, willing, spirited
              2. crippled, injured

gang   *n.*   crew, group, crowd, mob, company, band, troop

gangster   *n.*   member of a criminal gang, mobster, racketeer, bandit, ruffian, criminal

garment   *n.*   piece/item of apparel/clothing, item of dress

gasp   *v.*   gulp, pant, breathe with difficulty

gather   *v.*   assemble, collect, pick up, crop, reap, glean, combine, meet, congregate, convene

gaudy   *a.*   showy, flashy, garish, glaring, glossy, loud, lurid

gauge   *v.*   measure, estimate, assess, standardize, make uniform

gaunt   *a.*   lean, haggard, grim, cadaverous

gay   *a.*   joyful, joyous, happy, jolly, cheerful, merry, light-hearted, mirthful, carefree, sporting, playful, full of fun, gleeful, elated

gaze   *v.*   look at, regard intently/piercingly/fixedly

gear   *n.*   1. equipment, apparatus, tools, appliances, tackle, harness, clothing, apparel
              2. cog, toothed wheel

gem   *n.*   jewel, precious stone

general   *a.*   common, usual, ordinary, normal, standard, customary, widespread, not limited/particular/localized

generous   *a.*   1. liberal, freely-giving, magnanimous, munificent, not mean, unprejudiced
              2. ample, abundant, copious, fertile, plentiful, plenteous

genial   *a.*   cordial, jovial, friendly, pleasant, cheerful, sociable, kindly, agreeable, mild, warm, equable, enlivening

gentle   *a.*   1. soft, tender, light, mild, kind, quiet, tame, timid, moderate, gradual, manageable
              2. genteel, wellborn, of gentle birth, honorable

genuine	*a.*	real, true, not false/counterfeit/forged, authentic, sound, aboveboard, straight, pure, pedigree, purebred
germinate	*v.*	begin to grow, shoot, sprout, bud
gesture	*n.*	1. meaningful/significant movement of body/limb 2. indication/token of (some kind of emotion)
get	*v.*	gain, obtain, acquire, receive, win, come to own/possess, collect, glean, achieve, attain
ghastly	*a.*	1. pale, wan, white, lurid, ghostlike, unearthly, weird 2. horrible, frightful, dreadful, terrible, shocking, gruesome, grisly, hideous, repulsive, objectionable
ghost	*n.*	spirit, phantom, spectre, spook, wraith, soul, hallucination, apparition, vision, image
giant	*a.*	gigantic, unusually large/big/tall, great, huge, mammoth, immense, enormous, tremendous, monstrous, colossal
giddy	*a.*	1. dizzy, dazed, faint, inclined to fall/stagger, intoxicated 2. frivolous, flighty, fickle, excitable, inconstant
gift	*n.*	1. present, donation, deposit, bestowal, contribution, endowment, benefit, grant, allowance 2. talent, faculty, virtue
gigantic	*a.*	giant, massive, very big, great, huge, vast, tremendous, enormous, monstrous
give	*v.*	1. present, donate, bestow, contribute, endow, grant, award, allow, deliver, hand/make over, impart, confer, devote, dedicate, provide, allot, assign, hold out 2. collapse, break, bend, yield
glad	*a.*	1. pleased, happy, content, delighted, joyful ·'2. bright, beautiful, pleasing, happy, cheerful, joyous, festive
glamorous	*a.*	beautiful, pretty, attractive, charming, alluring, enchanting, bewitching
glance	*n.*	quick/momentary look, glimpse, flash, gleam, shaft
	v.	slide/glide/dart/bounce off, ricochet
glare	*n.*	1. dazzle, gleam, flash, fierce/bright light/flame/glow 2. fierce/fixed/angry look
gleam	*n.*	light, flash, dazzle, beam, flame, glow
glimpse	*n.*	quick/momentary look, glance
glisten	*v.*	shine, glitter, gleam, sparkle, flash, twinkle, shimmer
globe	*n.*	ball, orb, sphere, spheroid **globule:** *small ball, spheroid*
gloomy	*a.*	sad, cheerless, dull, glum, depressed, depressing, unhappy, dismal, downcast, dejected, melancholy, despondent, mournful, threatening, pessimistic, sullen, dark, dusky, dreary, cheerless, drab, not lit/illuminated
glorious	*a.*	delightful, splendid, wonderful, marvelous, magnificent, brilliant, famous, illustrious, praiseworthy, honorable

glossy   *a.*   shiny, gleaming, flashy, gaudy, garish

glow   *v.*   1. burn brightly, give/throw out light, emit light, incandescence
2. flush, blush, burn with ardor/passion, tingle

glue   *n.*   gum, paste, adhesive, fixative, mucilage, cement

glum   *a.*   sad, unhappy, dismal, gloomy, melancholy, downcast, dejected, cheerless, depressed, despondent, pessimistic

glutton   *n.*   greedy person, excessive eater, person with a great appetite, gourmand, voracious animal

go   *v.*   1. move/depart from, start, move off/away
2. journey, travel, proceed, progress, make way, pass into
3. pass, elapse
4. belong
5. be in motion/active/in action

goal   *n.*   aim, ambition, object, objective, intent, intention, target, purpose

good   *a.*   1. true, right, just, kind, gentle, saintly, worthy, virtuous, not corrupted, upright, righteous, generous, benevolent, philanthropic, superior, praiseworthy
2. favorable, beneficial, helpful, sound, wholesome, reliable, dependable, efficient, profitable, unadulterated, fresh, unblemished, untainted
3. skillful, talented, clever, able

   n.   welfare, betterment, advantage, interest

goods   *n.*   1. things owned, belongings, property
2. things for sale, merchandise, wares

gorge   *n.*   pass, narrow opening/neck between hills/mountains, mountain pass

   v.   eat/feed/devour greedily, fill, glut, distend, satiate

gorgeous   *a.*   magnificent, sumptuous, ornate, dazzling, lovely, brilliant, very colorful

gossip   *v.*   talk idly/lightly/foolishly/ unrestrainedly, chatter, prattle, prate, blab, tittle-tattle, spread news/rumors

govern   *v.*   control, rule, manage, conduct, guide, direct, administer, command, lead, influence, regulate, sway, determine, decide, curb, bridle

grab   *v.*   seize, snatch, clutch, rip, clasp, grasp, capture, arrest, take/appropriate greedily

graceful   *a.*   beautiful, beauteous, elegant, refined, charming, well-favored, attractive, pleasing, handsome, ornate

gracious   *a.*   courteous, polite, well-mannered, mannerly, kind, benevolent, agreeable, pleasing, condescending, indulgent

gradual   *a.*   slow, not quick/fast/rapid/ steep/sudden/abrupt, cautious, by degrees, bit by bit, little by little

grand   *a.*   great, big, large, elevated, immense, magnificent, splendid, superb, stately, gentlemanly, ladylike, dignified, renowned, celebrated, distinguished, important

grant	*v.*	give, donate, contribute, present, award, provide, concede, bestow, make available, allow, permit	

grasp   *v.*
1. seize, grab, snatch, clutch, clasp, grip, hold, take hold of, capture
2. know, understand, comprehend

grateful   *a.*   thankful, comforting, refreshing, acceptable, favorable, pleasing

great   *a.*   big, large, grand, huge, vast, immense, gigantic, tremendous, powerful, elevated, important, distinguished, famous, celebra ted, prominent, renowned, well-known, exalted, eminent

greedy   *a.*   avaricious, covetous, grasping, rapacious, gluttonous, piggish, voracious, ravenous

greet   *v.*   welcome, salute, hail, acknowledge, bid

grief   *n.*
1. sorrow, distress, sadness, woe, misery, heartache, regret, anguish, worry, mourning
2. misfortune, bad luck, trouble, failure, disaster

grip   *v.*   clutch, grasp, hold, clasp, seize, snatch, grab, capture, arrest

groan   *v.*   moan, cry with pain/sorrow, whimper, lament, sob, complain, grumble

groove   *n.*   channel, rut, trench, hollow

gross   *a.*
1. big, large, bulky, fat, obese, bloated, overfed
2. glaring, flagrant, palpable
3. total, whole, before/ without deductions, not net

ground   *n.*   earth, floor, base, foundation

group   *n.*
1. set, collection, selection, combination, assortment, class, cluster, number, quantity
2. crowd, company, gathering, assembly, gang, throng

grow   *v.*
1. get/become bigger/larger, enlarge, increase, expand, swell, amplify, stretch, arise, develop, flourish, spread
2. plant, cultivate, shoot, sprout, germinate, multiply, reproduce, proliferate, mature, ripen

growl   *v.*   snarl, mutter angrily, grumble, complain

grown-up   *a.*   grown, adult, mature

gruesome   *a.*   ghastly, horrible, horrifying, frightening, dreadful, hideous, grim, macabre, grisly, ugly, revolting, unearthly, terrible

grumble   *v.*   complain, dissent, speak/voice dissent, raise/make objections, growl, murmur, rumble

guarantee   *v.*   undertake, promise faithfully/truly, warrant, confirm, certify

guess   *v.*   estimate, suppose, suspect, surmise, imagine, conjecture, hazard, divine

guesswork: *conjecture, supposition*

guide   *v.*   lead, direct, escort, conduct, advise, counsel, instruct

guile	*n.*	deceit, treachery, trickery, cunning, slyness, craftiness, artfulness	
guilt	*n.*	crime, sin, wrongdoing, fault, culpability	
gullible	*a.*	easily deceived/tricked/cheated/taken in, too trustful/trusting, innocent, naive (naïve)	
gum	*n.*	glue, paste, adhesive, fixative, cement, mucilage	

gun	*n.*	weapon, firearm, pistol, revolver, automatic, cannon
gush	*n.*	outrush, fast flow (of liquid), stream
	v.	make a show of affection/tenderness, speak sentimentally/affectedly
gust	*n.*	1. wind, breeze, blast, squall
		2. burst of sound/smoke/flame/fire/rain/anger/passion

H h

habit   *n.*   custom, tradition, practice, rule, routine, procedure, fashion, vogue, mode

habitual   *a.*   customary, accustomed, usual, normal, regular, general, constant

haggard   *a.*   careworn, worn-out, gaunt, emaciated, drawn, tired, weary, exhausted, worried troubled

hail   *v.*   greet, salute, signal, acknowledge, call, shout for, acclaim, applaud, cheer

halt   *v.*   stop, arrest, hesitate, pause, rest, wait
   a.   lame, limping, crippled

hammer   *v.*   beat, knock, strike, pound, hit, drive, bang, rap, tap

hamper   *v.*   get in the way of, hinder, obstruct, impede, burden, handicap
   n.   large basket

handicap   *n.*   disadvantage, hindrance, disability, burden, obstruction, penalty
   v.   hinder, impede, obstruct, get in the way of, hamper, burden

handle   *v.*   1. deal with, undertake, manage, manipulate
2. hold, touch, feel
   n.   haft, knob

handsome   *a.*   fair, good-looking, beautiful, lovely, pretty graceful, elegant, comely

handy   *a.*   1. near/close by, within reach, useful, helpful, convenient
2. dexterous, adept, skillful, skilled, clever, talented, resourceful

hang   *v.*   suspend, drape, droop, dangle, swing

haphazard   *a.*   motley, jumbled, at random, by chance, unplanned

happen   *v.*   occur, come to pass, take place, chance, befall

happy   *a.*   delighted, contented, joyful, joyous, bright, glad, pleased, cheerful, cheery, jolly, merry, gleeful, gay, ecstatic, enrapt ured, lucky, fortunate
   happy-go-lucky: *easy-going, uncaring, friendly*

harass   *v.*   pester, plague, annoy, irritate, trouble, bother, badger

hard   *a.*   1. firm, solid, strong, unyielding, rigid, durable
2. stern, severe, harsh, unfeeling, insensitive, pitiless, callous, hard-hearted, exacting, unkind, unsympathetic
3. not easy, difficult
   hard-headed: *practical, business-like, shrewd, canny*

hardly   *adv.*   scarcely, with difficulty, only just

hardship   *n.*   misfortune, mishap, trouble, difficulty, burden, trial, handicap

hardy   *a.*   strong, sturdy, robust, hearty, vigorous, enduring

harm   *v.*   hurt, injure, damage, wrong, abuse, treat unfairly/unjustly

harmless   *a.*   not harmful/hurtful/damaging, inoffensive, innocent, innocuous

harsh   *a.*   1. rough, severe, strict, hard, unfeeling, insensitive, unkind, pitiless, callous, cruel, exacting
2. grating, jarring, rough, unpleasant, unmusical, sharp, piercing

harvest   *n.*   crop, yield, produce
           v.   gather, collect, crop

hasty   *a.*   1. quick, rapid, speedy, swift, fast
                2. abrupt, curt, reckless, rash, impetuous, precipitate, inconsiderate, thoughtless, hurried

hatch   *v.*   incubate, develop, emerge (from an egg)

hate   *v.*   dislike, abhor, loathe, detest, be averse to, despise

hateful   *a.*   detestable, abhorrent, loathsome, distasteful, obnoxious, revolting

haughty   *a.*   arrogant, overbearing, proud, snobbish, pompous, disdainful

haul   *v.*   pull, draw, drag, tow
          n.   catch (of fish), collection, drag, pull

haunt   *v.*   1. visit/call frequently
                2. follow, chase, dog, hound
          n.   favorite retreat/den

have   *v.*   possess, hold, own, secure, obtain, allow, permit, tolerate

hazard   *n.*   risk, danger, peril, menace, chance, gamble, venture

hazy   *a.*   1. misty, cloudy, foggy, dim, dull
                2. doubtful, vague, uncertain, indefinite, nebulous, obscure, confused, not clear

head   *n.*   1. chief, principal, leader, "boss"
                2. source, origin, top, upper end
                3. cranium, mind, brain, intelligence

headlong   *adv.*   1. head first, head forwards
                  2. hastily, rashly, recklessly, impetuously, abruptly, thoughtlessly

headstrong   *a.*   stubborn, obstinate, rash, reckless, willful, hot-headed

heal   *v.*   cure, treat, restore/bring back to health, mend, repair, remedy

healthy   *a.*   well, fit, strong, robust, vigorous, hearty, sound, wholesome, salubrious

heap   *n.*   pile, mound, stack, mass, load, collection, accumulation

hear   *v.*   listen to, give audience to

heart   *n.*   center, middle, core, crux, kernel

heartless   *a.*   unfeeling, insensitive, indifferent, uncaring, pitiless, callous, cruel, unkind, hard-hearted, exacting

hearty   *a.*   1. cordial, jovial, genial, friendly, good-natured, cheery, cheerful
                2. honest, true, sincere, not hypocritical
                3. strong, robust, sturdy

heat   *n.*   1. hotness, warmth, glow
                2. anger, fury, annoyance
                3. excitement, zeal, enthusiasm

heavy   *a.*   1. weighty, massive, ponderous, burdensome, cumbersome, sluggish, unyielding, laborious
                2. dull, downcast, gloomy, oppressive

hectic   *a.*   feverish, exciting, bustling, busy, panicky

hedge   *n.*   fence, barrier, enclosure
          v.   dodge, evade, avoid, prevaricate

heed   *v.*   notice, regard, attend, take note of, observe

hefty   *a.*   heavy, big, large, strong, powerful

help   *v.*   aid, assist, succor, support

herald	*n.*	messenger, announcer, forerunner	
	v.	proclaim, announce, usher in	
heroic	*a.*	brave, courageous, valiant, bold, fearless, gallant, daring, undaunted	
hesitate	*v.*	pause, waver, be reluctant, vacillate, falter, demur	
hide	*v.*	conceal, keep secret, cover, lurk, dissemble, disguise	
	n.	skin, pelt	
hideous	*a.*	ugly, horrible, horrid, revolting, frightful, ghastly	
high	*a.*	1. tall, steep, lofty, elevated 2. exalted, eminent 3. strong, shrill, keen **high-handed:** *arrogant, overbearing* **high-minded:** *noble, proud*	
hilarious	*a.*	funny, amusing, jolly, merry, gay	
hill	*n.*	small mountain, mount, mound, hillock	
hinder	*v.*	hamper, impede, delay, trammel, handicap, obstruct, block, check, stop	
hindmost	*a.*	last, end, rear, final	
hint	*n.*	roundabout/indirect suggestion, clue, inkling, implication	
hire	*v.*	employ (a person for wages), lend (a thing for a payment), engage, set on	
hit	*v.*	strike, beat, punch, thump, slap, clout, rap, tap, knock, hit, cuff, buffet	
hitch	*v.*	fasten, tie up, attach, tether	
	n.	1. fastening, tethering, tie 2. difficulty, problem, check, obstruction, hindrance	
hoard	*n.*	hidden/reserve store, hidden treasure, stockpile, collection, accumulation	

hoarse	*a.*	husky, gruff, harsh
hoax	*v.*	trick, fool, deceive, defraud, bamboozle, spoof, hoodwink, cheat
hold	*v.*	1. grasp, grab, clasp, seize, arrest, secure, slop 2. have, own, possess 3. believe, declare, proclaim
hole	*n.*	1. hollow, pit, cavity, indentation, bore, space 2. difficulty, fix, mess
holiday	*n.*	vacation, rest, excursion, leave, anniversary, furlough
hollow	*a.*	1. empty, not solid 2. not sincere, insincere, shallow, hypocritical, pretentious
	n.	hole, pit, cavity, indentation, concavity, crease, wrinkle, furrow, dell, valley
holy	*a.*	sacred, godly, revered, consecrated, blessed, divine, religious, devout, venerated
home	*n.*	dwelling, residence, abode
homely	*a.*	plain, simple, ordinary, commonplace, primitive, unpretentious, uncomely, not comely, homespun
honest	*a.*	true, upright, straight, open, aboveboard, straightforward, truthful, trustworthy, sincere, honorable, just, fair
honor	*n.*	good/sound/high/worthy reputation/rank, respect, esteem, renown, fame, glory
hoodwink	*v.*	cheat, deceive, trick, hoax, fool, bamboozle
hope	*v.*	expect, anticipate, wish, be ambitious
hopeless	*a.*	without hope, desperate, despairing, unpromising, impossible

horrible	a.	horrid, terrible, dreadful, hideous, awful, frightful, repulsive, loathsome, repugnant
horrify	v.	frighten, make afraid, shock, dismay, alarm, fill with dread/terror
hospitable	a.	kind, friendly, generous, accommodating, sociable, neighborly
host	n.	1. multitude, large crowd, swarm, army 2. hotel-keeper, innkeeper 3. entertainer (of guests)
hostile	a.	unfriendly, threatening, antagonistic, menacing
hot	a.	1. very warm, burning, glowing, aglow, fiery, blazing, ablaze, flaming, aflame 2. eager, hasty, quick **hot-tempered:** *quick-tempered, irascible*
house	n.	dwelling, shelter, abode
house	v.	shelter, protect, hold, contain
however	adv.	but, still, nevertheless, howsoever
hue	n.	tint, shade, color, complexion
hug	v.	clasp, embrace, cuddle, squeeze, press, cling, hold
huge	a.	large, big, great, giant, gigantic, enormous, vast, bulky, immense, monstrous, mammoth, tremendous, colossal
human	n.	human being, man, *Homo Sapiens*
humane	a.	kind, merciful, sympathetic, considerate, compassionate, gentle, tender
humble	a.	meek, modest, unimportant, unpretentious, unassuming, shy, retiring, reticent
humor	n.	1. amusement, fun 2. whim, fancy
	v.	pamper, spoil, agree with
hungry	a.	starving, famished, ravenous
hunt	v.	search, chase, course, pursue, track, trail, follow, quest, seek, trace
hurl	v.	throw, fling, eject, project, propel, heave, toss, sting, pitch, cast
hurry	v.	haste, hasten, speed, rush, scurry, dash
hurt	v.	injure, harm, pain, wound, maim, bruise, afflict, offend, grieve
hypocritical	a.	false, deceitful, insincere, two-faced

I i

icy   *a.*   1. ice-covered, frozen, frosty, frigid, cold
2. unfriendly, hostile, distant, chilly, cool

idea   *n.*   thought, notion, fancy, concept, impression, conjecture, plan, design, scheme

ideal   *a.*   perfect, absolute, visionary, faultless

identical   *a.*   exactly alike/the same, uniform, equivalent

identify   *v.*   know, recognize, pick out

idiotic   *a.*   stupid, foolish, silly, absurd, not sensible, nonsensical, crazy, stupid, irrational, illogical, ridiculous

idle   *a.*   1. lazy, sluggish, shiftless, unoccupied, inactive, unemployed
2. empty, vain, useless, pointless
3. uncultivated, unfilled, unused, barren

ignite   *v.*   set alight/on fire, light, take fire, burn, incinerate

ignorant   *a.*   without knowledge, uneducated, untutored, not learned, unlearned, uninstructed, illiterate

ignore   *v.*   disregard, refuse to notice, flout, scorn, pooh-pooh, boycott, cold-shoulder

     a.   1. sick, unwell, ailing, indisposed
2. bad, evil, malignant, malevolent
3. unlucky, unfortunate, unfavorable

ill-advised: *unwise, wrongly advised*

ill at ease: *uneasy, embarrassed, nervous*

ill-disposed: *unfriendly, hostile*

ill-favored: *ugly, plain, not comely*

ill-gotten: *dishonestly obtained*

ill health: *poor health, indisposition*

ill humor: *bad temper, moodiness*

ill-judged: *unwise, not circumspect*

ill-natured: *bad tempered, churlish*

ill will: *hatred, enmity, malevolence*

illegal   *a.*   unlawful, illegitimate, illicit, criminal, against the law

illness   *n.*   ill health, poor health, indisposition, sickliness, infirmity

illogical   *a.*   unreasonable, irrational, absurd

illuminate   *v.*   1. light, light up, shine upon, throw/cast light upon, brighten
2. enlighten

illusion   *n.*   deception, image, fantasy, dream, delusion

illustration   *n.*   1. picture, drawing
2. example, instance, case, specimen, model

imaginary   *a.*   not real, unreal, fanciful, fancied, pretended, make-believe, theoretical, hypothetical

imagine   *v.*   suppose, pretend, fancy, make believe

imitate   *v.*   copy, match, follow, reproduce, duplicate, mimic, ape, mock, impersonate

mmediately	*adv.*	now, at this time, promptly, without delay instantly, right away, at once, this instant, directly
mmense	*a.*	very large, great, enormous, huge, giant, gigantic, immense, tremendous, vast, mighty, colossal, monstrous
mmerse	*v.*	1. submerge, plunge, dip sink, douse, soak 2. be absorbed/engrossed in (a book)
mminent	*a.*	approaching, impending, threatening
mmortal	*a.*	undying, abiding, permanent, everlasting, eternal
mmovable	*a.*	1. fixed, rigid, solid, immobile 2. stubborn, obstinate, steadfast, resolute
mpact	*n.*	collision, contact, clash
mpart	*v.*	1. give, donate, make available, convey 2. tell, reveal, inform, instruct, advise
mpartial	*a.*	fair, just, unbiased, unprejudiced
mpatient	*a.*	not patient, restless, fidgety, fretful, fussy, eager, peevish, petulant
mpede	*v.*	hinder, handicap, hamper, restrict, obstruct, delay, oppose, block, check, arrest, frustrate, thwart, retard
mperfect	*a.*	incomplete, faulty, defective, blemished, tainted, damaged
mpertinent	*a.*	cheeky, saucy, audacious, impudent, forward, rude, bold, impolite, discourteous, brazen, insolent
mpetuous	*a.*	hasty, rash, reckless, abrupt, precipitate, unthinking, headstrong
implore	*v.*	beg, beseech, entreat, pray
imply	*v.*	hint, suggest, give a clue/inkling, infer
impolite	*a.*	rude, discourteous, uncivil, unmannerly, bad-mannered, ill-mannered, disrespectful, impertinent, cheeky, saucy, impudent
important	*a.*	1. significant, of moment/consequence, essential, urgent, vital, imperative, pressing, outstanding, momentous, memorable 2. illustrious, notable, prominent, famous, celebrated, eminent
impose	*v.*	put/place/lay on/upon, tax, take advantage
imposing	*a.*	great, grand, fine, impressive, awe-inspiring, awesome, striking, splendid, mighty, majestic, noble, stately
impressive	*a.*	great, imposing, awe-inspiring, awesome, striking, stirring, moving, thrilling, exciting, notable
impromptu	*a.*	unprepared, unrehearsed, off-hand, spontaneous
improper	*a.*	not proper/correct, wrong, incorrect, unsuitable, unsatisfactory, unbecoming, indecent, unseemly
improve	*v.*	make/become better, amend
imprudent	*a.*	unwise, ill-advised, rash, reckless
impudent	*a.*	audacious, impertinent, cheeky, saucy, rude, forward, disrespectful, brazen, bold, flippant
impulsive	*a.*	impatient, hasty, reckless, rash, impetuous, precipitate, unthinking, thoughtless, careless
impure	*a.*	not pure, adulterated, unclean, tainted, foul, dirty

inadequate	*a.*	unsatisfactory, insufficient, unsuitable, deficient
inappropriate	*a.*	unsuitable, inadequate, unsatisfactory, unbecoming, improper, unseemly
incessant	*a.*	unceasing, without ceasing, continual, constant, unending, endless, perpetual, ceaseless, eternal
incident	*n.*	event, happening, occurrence, affair, occasion, episode
incompetent	*a.*	incapable, unqualified, unfit, deficient
incorrect	*a.*	wrong, unsuitable, faulty, unsatisfactory, inappropriate, inadequate, inaccurate, erroneous, improper
increase	*v.*	make/become larger/greater, enlarge, grow, multiply, gain, extend, expand, swell, raise
incredible	*a.*	surprising, amazing, astounding, hard to believe/accept/understand
indecent	*a.*	coarse, disgusting, rude, vulgar, uncouth, improper, unseemly, unbecoming
indeed	*adv.*	in truth/reality, really, truly, for certain, certainly
indefinite	*a.*	uncertain, unsure, vague, ambiguous, undecided, undefined, unfixed, unclear
independent	*a.*	free, at liberty, alone, uncontrolled, separate, self-sufficient, self-reliant
indicate	*v.*	point out, show, mark, hint, tell, designate
indifferent	*a.*	1. uninterested, unconcerned, tolerant 2. mediocre, moderate, passable
indignation	*n.*	resentment, anger, annoyance
indirect	*a.*	not direct, roundabout, circuitous
indispensable	*a.*	essential, necessary, much needed, required
indistinct	*a.*	dim, dull, blurred, misty, hazy, nebulous, vague, uncertain, confused, indefinite, obscure
industrious	*a.*	busy, hard-working, active, diligent
ineffective	*a.*	useless, vain, idle, powerless, ineffectual, inadequate
inevitable	*a.*	certain, sure, inescapable, unavoidable
inferior	*a.*	1. lower, below 2. poor, poorer, mediocre, second-rate
infinite	*a.*	boundless, limitless, endless, countless, immeasurable, unlimited, eternal, immense
infirm	*a.*	1. feeble, frail, weak, ailing 2. unsound, unstable
inflame	*v.*	set alight/ablaze
inflate	*v.*	expand, distend, swell, dilate, puff up
influence	*v.*	affect, sway, persuade, direct, control, guide, lead
inform	*v.*	tell, make known to, advise
infrequent	*a.*	irregular, unusual, uncommon, rare
infuriate	*v.*	anger, vex, annoy, enrage, make furious, madden, incense, inflame
ingenious	*a.*	clever, gifted, talented, skillful, inventive
inhabit	*v.*	live/abide/reside/dwell/stay/lodge in, occupy
inhuman	*a.*	not human/like a human, brutal, bestial, inhumane
injure	*v.*	hurt, harm, maim, wound, damage

inkling	*n.*	suggestion, hint, whisper, suspicion
innocent	*a.*	without guilt/fault, not guilty/at fault, guiltless, faultless, blameless, harmless, innocuous, naïve (naive)
inquire	*v.*	ask, question, investigate, seek knowledge
inquisitive	*a.*	curious, inquiring, prying
insecure	*a.*	unsafe, unguarded
insignificant	*a.*	little, small, trivial, petty, trifling, unimportant, of no consequence, inconsequential
insolent	*a.*	impudent, impertinent, cheeky, saucy, rude, insulting, offensive, defiant
inspect	*v.*	examine, check, investigate
instant	*a.*	urgent, pressing, prompt, immediate
	n.	moment, present month/time
instruct	*v.*	1. teach, train, coach, tutor 2. order, command, direct, guide, inform, tell, advise
insufficient	*a.*	inadequate, scanty, meager, not enough
insult	*v.*	offend, cheek, abuse, be insolent/impertinent/impudent/rude to
intact	*a.*	1. complete, whole, perfect, sound 2. undamaged, unhurt, uninjured, unharmed, unbroken
intelligent	*a.*	sensible, alert, shrewd, astute, well-informed
intention	*n.*	intent, aim, purpose, goal, object, plan, idea, motive
intentional	*a.*	intended, deliberate, premeditated
internal	*a.*	inner, inside, interior
interval	*n.*	pause, gap, break, recess
intricate	*a.*	complicated, complex, involved, tricky, difficult
intrude	*v.*	enter uninvited, encroach, invade
invade	*v.*	intrude, enter, encroach
invasion	*n.*	encroachment, intrusion
invalid	*a.*	valueless, worthless
invalid	*n.*	sick/ailing/convalescent person
invent	*v.*	devise, make up, create, concoct, design, conceive, fabricate, plan, fashion, discover, originate
investigate	*v.*	inquire into, ask/question about, inspect, examine, check, search
irate	*a.*	angry, annoyed, vexed, furious, enraged
irksome	*a.*	tedious, tiresome, wearisome, boring, frustrating, irritating, perturbing
irritable	*a.*	fretful, peevish, petulant, easily annoyed/vexed/exasperated
irritate	*v.*	1. annoy, vex, exasperate, aggravate, provoke, bother, trouble, disturb 2. itch, chafe, make sore

J j

jab   *n.*   poke, stab, thrust, hit, abrupt/sudden/sharp/quick blow, punch

jabber   *v.*   chatter, babble, gab, gabble, gibber, speak/talk quickly/ incessantly/wildly/ senselessly/foolishly/ incoherently

jade   *v.*   tire, fatigue, wear out, make feel inferior

        a.   She felt quite **jaded** at the end of the day's work.

jagged   *a.*   rough, rough-edged, coarse, barbed, toothed, notched, crooked

jail   *n.*   prison, penitentiary, reformatory, dungeon

jam   *v.*   squeeze, crush, wedge in, crowd tightly together, block, fill up, make a stoppage, cram

        n.   1. squeeze, crush, blockage, stoppage, crowd

               2. conserve, preserve, confection

jangle   *v.*   sound harshly/noisily, clatter, clank, make bell-like sounds

jar   *v.*   jolt, grate, scrape, shake, bump, jerk, push, knock, move, jiggle, joggle, jostle, vibrate, throb, resound, sound harshly/discordantly, send shocks through

        n.   pot, urn, vase, pitcher, jug, vessel

jaunt   *n.*   outing, excursion, expedition, journey for pleasure
We took a **jaunt** to the beach in August.

jealous   *a.*   envious, grudging, resentful, distrustful, mistrustful, suspicious, intolerant

jeer   *v.*   sneer, taunt, gibe (jibe), deride, scoff, mock, make fun of, poke fun at, laugh at, joke about, ridicule, chaff, flout

jerk   *v.*   yank, pull, push, tug, thrust, nudge, snatch, jump, jolt, jig, jiggle, jog, joggle, twist, twitch, tremble, vibrate, move

jest   *v.*   joke, banter, taunt, scoff, chaff, ridicule, make/poke fun, quip, gag, speak/act amusingly/playfully/ funnily/comically/with humor, trifle

jewel   *n.*   1. precious stone, gem

               2. invaluable/precious/useful/ greatly loved/much esteemed person/thing

jig   *n.*   brisk/quick/rapid/lively dance, jump, skip, gallop, up-and-down movement/ motion, jog, jiggle, shake

jingle   *n.*   1. tinkle, clink, bell-like sound, chain-like noise, jangle

               2. little/popular/well-known/ easily-remembered/lively rhyme

jittery   *a.*   nervous, afraid, fearful, frightened, scared, timid, jumpy, worried, anxious, apprehensive

job   *n.*   1. task, piece of work

               2. business, employment, occupation, profession, post, trade, work, vocation

jog   *v.*   1. shake, push, jerk, jolt, nudge, thrust

               2. jig, dance, trot, trudge, walk unsteadily, travel slowly, go forward laboriously

join	*v.*	1. unite, combine, fasten, blend, merge, amalgamate, bind, marry 2. enroll, participate, enter
joke	*v.*	jest, gag, banter, quip, gibe (jibe), make/poke fun, banter, chaff, scoff, speak/act amusingly/with humor/playfully/funnily/comically, trifle
jolly	*a.*	cheerful, happy, gay, joyful, joyous, mirthful, merry, festive, jovial, jocular, full of fun, amusing, lively, plea.sant
jolt	*n.*	jerk, bump, sudden/abrupt/sharp blow, knock, jog, nudge
jot	*n.*	trifle, dot, tiny fragment
	v.	write down, make quick/rough notes
journey	*n.*	trip, voyage, expedition, excursion, distance travelled/traversed
jovial	*a.*	cheerful, happy, gay, merry, mirthful, jocular, good-humored, good-natured, full of fun, pleasant, festive
joy	*n.*	delight, happiness, joyfulness, joyousness, merriment, glee, jubilance, gladness, felicity, jollity, bliss, great pleasure, jubilation
jubilant	*a.*	joyful, delighted, glad, very happy, rejoicing, exultant. triumphant

judge	*v.*	assess, estimate, decide, form opinion about, suppose, consider, form/make/give judgement, criticize, censure, act as a judge, try, adjudicate, pass sentence on
jumble	*v.*	mix up, muddle, confuse, disarrange, disarray, throw into disorder
	n.	junk, oddments, discarded clothes/objects
jump	*v.*	leap, spring, skip, gambol, jig, jog, move up and down, start, move, wince, twitch, shake, jolt, jerk
junk	*n.*	jumble, oddments, waste, rubbish, discarded objects
just	*a.*	fair, impartial, right, true, aboveboard, honest, straight, correct, proper, suitable, fitting, deserved, equitable, righteous, upright
	adv.	exactly, precisely, truly, quite, barely, only, then, at that time, now, at this time, very recently
justice	*n.*	1. fairness, rightness, impartiality, fair treatment, just conduct, equity, lawful/legal authority 2. magistrate, judge
jut	*v.*	stick out, project, protrude
juvenile	*n.*	child, youngster, young person, minor

K k

keen   *a.*   1. sharp, sharp-edged, cutting, piercing, biting, bitter, penetrating, acute, quick, quick-witted, alert, sensitive, intense, vivid, acute

                   2. zealous, enthusiastic, willing, eager, ardent, fervent, earnest, much interested, zestful, vigorous, active, busy, industrious

keep   *v.*   hold, retain, save, possess, look after, preserve, guard, maintain, protect, detain, reserve, have charge of, adhere to, observe, pay regard to, be true to, stand by, remain, stay

kidnap   *v.*   abduct, carry off by force, take away (a person), steal (a child)

kill   *v.*   murder, slay, slaughter, massacre, butcher, put to death, put an end to, cause the death of, harm fatally/mortally, destroy, liquidate, execute, assassinate, exterminate

kin   *n.*   kindred, kinsfolk, kith, family, relatives, relations, group, tribe, race

                   akin: *alike, similar, of the same group/tribe/race*

kind   *n.*   type, sort, variety, quality, character, nature, category, class, classification, group, family, kin, kindred, tribe, race

          a.   kind-hearted, considerate, thoughtful, gentle, tender, loving, affectionate, friendly, benevolent, philanthropic, good, courteous

king   *n.*   ruler, monarch, sovereign, His Majesty

kingdom   *n.*   realm, domain, dominion

kit   *n.*   set, outfit, equipment, tools, apparatus

knack   *n.*   art, skill, dexterity, ability, faculty, cleverness, trick, habit, method, means, technique

knock   *v.*   strike, rap on/at, hit, tap

          n.   punch, bump, bang, thud

knot   *v.*   tie, tangle, rope together, link, join, unite, marry

know   *v.*   1. have knowledge of, be aware of, understand, comprehend, realize, have learned, be versed in, be informed about

                   2. be acquainted with, be intimate with, recognize, be able to distinguish, identify, be certain/sure of

                   know-it-all: *one who professes/pretends to know everything*

                   know-how: *special skill, expertise*

knowing   *a.*   knowledgeable, well-informed, shrewd, astute, cunning, artful, sharp, wide-awake, cute, intelligent, clever

knowledge   *n.*   learning, understanding, information, intelligence, experience

L l

label	*n.*	1. title, name, mark, stamp 2. tag, seal
labor	*n.*	work, toil, task, effort, exertion, industry, employment
laborious	*a.*	tiring, fatiguing, wearisome, toilsome, exhausting, exacting, painstaking, hard, heavy, tough, difficult, industrious, diligent
lack	*v.*	be without, be deprived/deficient in, short/in want of, require, need
lag	*v.*	linger, dawdle, loiter, straggle, delay
lame	*a.*	1. limping, crippled, injured 2. unsatisfactory, poor, inadequate, imperfect
land	*n.*	1. earth, ground 2. country, territory, region 3. estate, farm, holding
	v.	get/go ashore/on shore/land, beach
large	*a.*	big, great, grand, huge, enormous, massive, giant, gigantic, bulky, vast, spacious, monstrous, abundant, ample, plentiful
last	*a.*	1. end, final, hindmost, terminal, concluding 2. latest, most recent
	v.	hold out, endure, persist, stay, remain
lasting	*a.*	enduring, permanent, perpetual, durable, stable, steady, constant
late	*a.*	1. behind time, overdue, tardy, delayed, slow 2. deceased, departed, dead 3. past, recent
laugh	*v.*	guffaw, chuckle, exult, scoff **laugh at:** *make fun of, ridicule, scoff at*
laughable	*a.*	amusing, funny, comic, comical, mirth-provoking, humorous
lavish	*a.*	liberal, generous, extravagant, open-handed, munificent, bountiful
lawful	*a.*	legal, legitimate, permissible, permitted/allowed by law
lawless	*a.*	disorderly, unruly, rebellious, uncontrollable, uncontrolled, unmanageable
lax	*a.*	easy, easy-going, loose, slack, negligent, careless, unmindful
layer	*n.*	film, deposit, stratum, seam, thickness
lazy	*a.*	idle, indolent, sluggish, lethargic, slothful
lead	*v.*	1. guide, conduct, escort, control, direct, steer, command 2. excel, surpass, be in front/advance/ahead
leader	*n.*	guide, head, chief, captain, commander, director, conductor, controller, master, boss
leak	*v.*	escape, run/pass/flow out, come out slowly/gradually, transpire
lean	*v.*	incline, slant, slope, bend, rest
	a.	thin, lank, lanky, slender, skinny
leap	*v.*	jump, spring, bound, vault, skip, gambol, caper
learned	*a.*	wise, well-informed, scholarly, well-educated
learning	*n.*	knowledge, education, scholarship

leave	*v.*	1. depart, quit, go away/out, vacate, desert, forsake
		2. will, bequeath
	n.	1. permission, consent
		2. holiday, absence, vacation, furlough
left	*a.*	left-hand, left-hand side
legal	*a.*	lawful, legitimate, allowed/permitted by law, permissible
legend	*n.*	story, tale, myth, fable, fiction
legendary	*a.*	mythical, fabulous, fanciful, fictitious, imaginary, marvelous, wonderful
legitimate	*a.*	1. lawful, legal, allowed/permitted by law, permissible
		2. true, real, authentic, proper, genuine, regular, acceptable, admissible
leisure	*n.*	spare/free time, ease, comfort, relaxation, rest
lengthen	*v.*	make longer, stretch, extend, increase
lenient	*a.*	mild, gentle, easy, easygoing, merciful
lessen	*v.*	lower, diminish, reduce, shorten, decrease
let	*v.*	allow, permit, tolerate
level	*a.*	flat, horizontal, even, smooth, straight, regular
	v.	knock down, raze, demolish
liberate	*v.*	set free/loose, release, give freedom to, discharge
lie	*v.*	1. lay, rest, recline, be recumbent
		2. tell an untruth/falsehood, fib, dissemble
lift	*v.*	raise, hoist, elevate
	n.	help, aid, assistance, support

light	*v.*	illuminate, ignite, set/on fire, afire
	a.	gentle, flimsy, frail, of little weight
lighten	*v.*	1. light up, brighten, clear, illuminate
		2. lessen/reduce/diminish load/burden/weight, make less heavy, ease, relieve
like	*v.*	love, approve of, be pleased with
	a.	alike, similar, resembling
limit	*n.*	border, boundary, edge, barrier, restriction, check, restraint, end, curtailment, curb, control
limp	*a.*	not stiff/rigid, flabby, slack, flaccid, drooping, loose, lax
	v.	walk awkwardly/lamely
linger	*v.*	delay, hang about, persist, tarry, dawdle, loiter, dally, lag
link	*v.*	connect, join, attach, bind, tie, unite, couple, knot, fasten, fix
list	*n.*	roll, register, record, inventory, tally, catalog, manifest, table
	v.	lean to one side
listen	*v.*	hear, attend
listless	*a.*	weary, tired, fatigued, slack, limp, languid, feeble, drooping
litter	*n.*	jumble, rubbish, waste, refuse
little	*a.*	small, tiny, diminutive, wee, minute
	n.	small quantity/amount/piece, morsel, bit, scrap
	adv.	not much/a lot, slightly
live	*v.*	1. exist, be alive
		2. dwell, reside, stay, remain, lodge, inhabit, abide

live	*a.*	1. active, viable
		2. glowing, unexploded
lively	*a.*	1. active, brisk, nimble, alive, spritely, vigorous, spirited
		2. cheerful, gay, jolly, merry, joyful, bright, brilliant, vivid
loath	*a.*	unwilling, reluctant
loathe	*v.*	hate, abhor, dislike intensely, detest, despise
locate	*v.*	place, put, site, situate
lofty	*a.*	1. high, elevated, towering
		2. conceited, haughty, proud, aloof
loiter	*v.*	hang about, linger, dawdle, dally, delay, lag, tarry
lonely	*a.*	lone, alone, lonesome, forlorn, companionless, isolated, desolate
long	*a.*	lengthy, extended, prolonged, far-reaching
	v.	desire, yearn, crave
look	*v.*	1. regard, observe, behold, eye, watch, examine, inspect, peep, glance, view, stare, gaze
		2. search, seek
		3. seem, appear
lose	*v.*	1. miss, mislay, drop
		2. fail, be defeated/ beaten/unsuccessful

lot	*n.*	1. all, every one, total number/quantity/amount, much, many
		2. item, article
		3. luck, fortune, fate, chance, destiny
loud	*a.*	1. noisy, blaring, deafening, discordant, tumultuous, clamorous, boastful, bombastic
		2. gaudy, glossy, vivid, bright, glaring
love	*v.*	like, hold dear, be fond of, be devoted to, cherish, adore
lovely	*a.*	beautiful, attractive, charming, pleasing, delightful, fine, lovable
loyalty	*n.*	faithfulness, devotion, fidelity, constancy
luck	*n.*	fortune, fate, lot, chance, destiny, success
lucky	*a.*	fortunate, favored
lull	*v.*	soothe, quiet, placate, calm
lurk	*v.*	hide, be concealed, lie in wait, prowl, skulk, sneak
lustrous	*a.*	bright, shining, radiant, splendid, brilliant, glossy
luxuriant	*a.*	rich, rank, prolific, profuse, lush, abundant, dense, thick
luxury	*n.*	costliness, wealth, opulence, affluence

M m

macabre   *a.*   grim, hideous, grisly, gruesome

mad   *a.*
1. insane, mentally ill/sick, deranged, frenzied
2. angry, annoyed, furious, enraged, irate

magazine   *n.*
1. warehouse, storehouse, store
2. periodical, journal

magic   *n.*
1. witchcraft, wizardry, sorcery, devilry
2. conjuring, legerdemain, sleight-of-hand, juggling

magnificent   *a.*   grand, superb, splendid, wonderful, marvelous, sumptuous

magnify   *v.*   make/become larger/bigger/greater, increase, enlarge, expand, exaggerate, amplify

maid   *n.*   maiden, girl, lass, wench, miss, damsel

mail   *n.*
1. postal service, letter post
2. letters, correspondence

maim   *v.*   injure, wound, disable, cripple, hurt, mutilate, mangle, crush, disfigure

main   *a.*   principal, most important, chief, central
   n.   **might and main:** *physical force/strength/power*

maintain   *v.*
1. keep, provide for, sustain, uphold, support, preserve
2. claim, hold, insist

majestic   *a.*   stately, regal, royal, grand, noble, magnificent, splendid, dignified

major   *a.*
1. greater, larger, more important, senior, superior
2. army/military officer

majority   *n.*
1. greater part/portion/number/fraction, bulk, most
2. adulthood

make   *v.*
1. do, perform, create, devise, fabricate, manufacture, construct, erect
2. compel, force
make-believe: *false, sham, pretended, imitation, bogus*

malady   *n.*   ailment, illness, sickness, disease, fever, ill health, indisposition, complaint

male   *n.*   man, boy, masculine animal

mammoth   *a.*   giant, gigantic, huge, immense, enormous, colossal
   n.   mastodon

man   *n.*
1. male, gentleman
2. employee, workman, hand
3. mankind, humanity, human race, *Homo Sapiens*

manage   *v.*
1. control, direct, run, organize, regulate, govern, administer
2. make do, get by/along

manageable   *a.*   controllable, disciplined, orderly, docile, timid, tame, gentle, quiet, obedient

manhood   *n.*   manliness, adulthood, maturity

mankind   *n.*   man, humans, humanity, human race

manly   *a.*   strong, virile, brave, bold, courageous, noble

manner   *n.*
1. way, method, approach, technique
2. style, mode, fashion, kind, sort, form

mannerism	*n.*	habit, trick, style, gesture, distinctive manner
manners	*n.*	behavior, conduct, habits, courtesy, politeness, etiquette, civility
manual	*n.*	handbook, instruction book, guide
	a.	by hand, done with the hands
manufacture	*v.*	make, construct, produce, fabricate, build
many	*a.*	a lot of, numerous, plenty, various
map	*n.*	chart, plan, diagram, outline
march	*v.*	walk/move in step, pace, pound
margin	*n.*	edge, border, boundary, rim, brink, limit
marine	*a.*	sea, nautical, maritime, oceanic
mark	*n.*	1. token, sign, indication, symbol, label, imprint, impression, brand, stamp
		2. stain, scar, blemish, smudge, speck, spot, blotch
	v.	1. observe, pay regard/attention to, attend to, notice, note, watch
		2. point at, indicate, label
market	*n.*	fair, bazaar, store, shops, shopping center
marketable	*a.*	saleable, commercial
maroon	*v.*	abandon (e.g., on an uninhabited island), desert, leave behind, isolate
marry	*v.*	tie, join, unite, bind, wed
marsh	*n.*	swamp, bog, morass, mire, fen, quagmire, slough
marvelous	*a.*	wonderful, amazing, extraordinary, unbelievable, delightful, splendid, superb

masculine	*a.*	male, manly, strong, virile, robust
mask	*v.*	disguise, hide, conceal, cover
mass	*n.*	1. quantity, amount, weight, body, bulk, size
		2. crowd, crush, mob
massacre	*v.*	slaughter, slay, kill, destroy, liquidate, butcher, put to death
massive	*a.*	ponderous, enormous, very large/big/heavy/bulky, giant, gigantic, huge, unwieldy
master	*n.*	1. employer, controller, head, chief, boss, director, leader
		2. expert, teacher, instructor
	v.	overcome, overpower, gain control/command of, subdue, tame, conquer
mastery	*n.*	control, command, power, supremacy, knowledge, grasp, understanding, skill, proficiency
masticate	*v.*	chew, grind
mat	*n.*	small rug/carpet, pad
	a.	matt, coarse, rough
	v.	tangle, twist
match	*v.*	1. be alike/the same, blend, harmonize, agree, tally, fit
		2. equal, overcome, oppose
	n.	1. wedding, marriage
		2. equal
		3. contest, game, competition
		4. wooden splint
material	*n.*	1. substance, matter
		2. facts, information, data
		3. cloth, fabric
	a.	1. real, actual, substantial, vital, essential, relevant, important
		2. worldly, earthly

matter	*n.*	1. substance, material
		2. happening, occurrence, event, topic, episode, affair, business, question
		3. pus
	v.	count, signify, be relevant/important
		matter-of-fact: *calm, down-to-earth, unemotional, nonchalant*
mature	*a.*	ripe, ready, full-grown, grown-up
maximum	*a.*	greatest, largest, biggest, most, utmost, supreme, highest
maybe	*adv.*	perhaps, possibly, by chance
		maze
	n.	labyrinth, puzzle, riddle
	v.	puzzle, bewilder, baffle, perplex, mystify
meager	*a.*	poor, small, trifling, slight, slim, scanty, limited, sparse, mean, niggardly
mean	*a.*	1. poor, small, meager, scanty, niggardly, trifling, stingy, ungenerous, miserly
		2. coarse, common, vulgar, nasty, base, vile, spiteful, unkind
		3. middle, average
	v.	1. intend, aim
		2. signify, indicate, show, convey
meaning	*n.*	explanation, definition, sense, significance, substance, intention, aim, object, purpose, point
meaningless	*a.*	without meaning, nonsensical, senseless, absurd, idiotic, pointless, useless
means	*n.*	1. method, way, technique, device, artifice, process
		2. money, wealth, possessions

measure	*v.*	determine/find the size of, assess, estimate, gauge
	n.	1. estimate, dimension, size
		2. measuring-instrument, gauge, ruler
mechanical	*a.*	1. machine-like, automatic, robot-like, of machines/machinery
		2. blind, unthinking, instinctive
mechanism	*n.*	machine, works, device
meddle	*v.*	interfere, pry, tamper, intervene, busybody
meek	*a.*	mild, timid, tame, docile, gentle, shy, humble, lowly, modest, retiring, reticent, unassuming
meet	*v.*	1. encounter, confront, come face to face
		2. join, unite, converge, come together, assemble, muster, gather, congregate, convene
		3. satisfy, fulfill, fill, answer
	a.	proper, correct, appropriate
melancholy	*a.*	sad, unhappy, dismal, gloomy, dejected, sorrowful, depressed, despondent, distressed, mournful, downcast, plaintive, melancholic
mellow	*a.*	1. ripe, juicy, soft, sweet, delicate, mature, perfect
		2. friendly, sociable, genial, cordial
member	*n.*	1. limb, organ, part
		2. entrant, affiliate, fellow, associate
memorize	*v.*	commit to memory, learn by heart
menace	*n.*	threat, danger, peril, hazard
mend	*v.*	repair, restore, correct, improve, adjust, rectify, overhaul, fix, patch, sew, stitch, darn

mental	*a.*	of the mind/brain/intellect, intellectual
mention	*v.*	name, nominate, speak of/about, refer to, state, declare, tell
	n.	notice, reference, statement, nomination
merchant	*n.*	trader, dealer, factor
mercy	*n.*	forgiveness, leniency, pity, compassion, sympathy, humanity, kindness
merge	*v.*	come together, join, unite, mix, blend, mingle, combine, be absorbed
merit	*v.*	deserve, earn, win
merry	*a.*	happy, gay, carefree, jolly, joyful, festive, jovial, cheerful, hilarious, vivacious
mess	*n.*	disorder, muddle, mix-up, confusion, jumble, litter, rubbish, dirt
method	*n.*	1. way, manner, means, process, technique, approach
		2. order, orderliness, system, arrangement
methodical	*a.*	orderly, systematic, significant, purposeful
middle	*a.*	mid, midway, mean, central
might	*n.*	energy, force, power, strength, intensity, vigor, greatness
mild	*a.*	1. meek, timid, inoffensive, shy, soft, smooth, gentle, light, calm, placid, easy, kind
		2. warm, fine, sunny
military	*a.*	soldierly, soldier-like, martial
	n.	army
mime	*v.*	mimic, imitate
mimic	*v.*	imitate, copy, ape, mock

mind	*n.*	brain, intellect, understanding
	v.	1. take care of, guard, watch, keep, look after
		2. heed, attend/pay regard to, obey
		3. remember, recollect, recall
		4. object to
mindful	*a.*	heedful, attentive, observant, aware, watchful
mine	*n.*	1. pit, shaft, colliery
		2. bomb
miniature	*a.*	small, tiny, petite, model, toy
minimum	*a.*	least, smallest, lowest
minor	*a.*	smaller, lesser, less important, lower, junior
	n.	juvenile, youngster, child
minority	*n.*	smaller part/portion/ number/fraction, least
minus	*a.*	less, without, short of, negative
minute	*a.*	very/extremely small/little/ tiny, insignificant
miraculous	*a.*	marvelous, wonderful, amazing, astounding, astonishing, surprising, magical, divine
mirror	*n.*	looking-glass, reflector
	v.	reflect, copy, imitate
mirth	*n.*	merriment, gaiety, jollity, glee, fun, amusement, laughter, hilarity
miscellaneous	*a.*	varied, various, mixed, assorted, mingled, diverse, divers, sundry
mischief	*n.*	1. naughtiness, willfullness, pranks
		2. damage, injury, destruction, vandalism
misconduct	*n.*	bad conduct/behavior, misbehavior, disorder

miserable	*a.*	sad, unhappy, gloomy, melancholy, doleful, depressed, dejected, despondent, sorrowful, woeful, mournful
misfortune	*n.*	bad/ill fortune/luck, difficulty, disaster, calamity
miss	*v.*	1. overlook, neglect, skip, lose, omit, leave out, avoid, fail to go/attend/hit 2. notice/regret the loss/absence of
	n.	girl, young lady/woman, lass, unmarried woman, spinster
mission	*n.*	task, duty, expedition, errand, assignment, purpose
mist	*n.*	fog, cloud, haze, moisture, dew, vapor
mistake	*n.*	error, fault, defect, flaw
mix	*v.*	combine, blend, mingle, unite, join
mob	*n.*	crowd, rabble, mass
	v.	crowd, crush, overwhelm, jostle, molest
mobile	*a.*	moving, quick, active, movable, portable
mock	*a.*	sham, imitation, false, fake, counterfeit
	v.	make fun of, deride, scoff, jeer, laugh at, tease, mimic, imitate
model	*n.*	1. example, specimen, prototype, pattern, figure, design 2. small/miniature/toy copy/version
	v.	make, mold, shape, fashion, form, design, plan
moderate	*a.*	fair, reasonable, not extreme, restrained
moderate	*v.*	soothe, pacify, placate, soften, control, reduce, check, curb
modern	*a.*	new, up-to-date, current, recent
modest	*a.*	meek, shy, retiring, reticent, humble, unassuming
moist	*a.*	damp, wet, humid
molest	*v.*	pester, interfere with, disturb, bother, trouble, annoy, worry
moment	*n.*	1. instant, second, flash 2. importance
monarch	*n.*	ruler, sovereign, king, queen, emperor, empress
monotonous	*a.*	unchanging, regular, dull, tedious, boring, uninteresting, wearisome
monster	*n.*	terrifying animal/beast, cruel/barbarous/inhuman man
moody	*a.*	sullen, sulky, peevish
mope	*v.*	fret, sulk, be listless/ discontented/dispirited
moral	*a.*	well-conducted, good, upright, ethical, virtuous, pious, honest, honorable, respectable
morale	*n.*	spirit, confidence, cheerfulness
moreover	*adv.*	what is more, furthermore, besides, also, in addition, additionally
morsel	*n.*	small piece, bit, fragment, shred, scrap
motion	*n.*	1. movement, action, disturbance 2. proposal, suggestion
motionless	*a.*	without motion/action, still, stationary, not moving
mount	*v.*	1. climb, go up, rise, ascend, get on, bestride (a horse or bicycle) 2. place, set, fix, display
	n.	hill, hillock, mound

mourn   *v.*   grieve, lament, sorrow

move   *v.*   1. carry, transfer
                      2. move place/position, travel, stir, shift
                      3. touch, arouse, agitate, excite
                      4. propose, suggest, recommend
    n.   step, act, action, decision

multiply   *v.*   increase, make/become greater/more, reproduce

multitude   *n.*   crowd, throng, mass

murder   *v.*   kill, slaughter, slay, have put to death, destroy, liquidate

must   *v.*   should, ought, are compelled/obliged to

musty   *a.*   stale, moldy, sour, fetid

mutiny   *v.*   disobey, revolt, rebel, riot
    n.   revolt, rebellion, uprising

mutter   *v.*   murmur, mumble, growl, grumble, complain, whisper

mystery   *n.*   puzzle, enigma, riddle, secret

myth   *n.*   story, tale, fable, legend

N n

nag   *v.*   give no peace to, pester, scold/find fault with persistently/regularly, chide, reprove

naked   *a.*   nude, bare, unclothed, uncovered, undressed, exposed, bald

name   *n.*   1. title, label, appellation, term
2. reputation
   v.   nominate, mention, speak of

nap   *n.*   short sleep, doze, siesta, snooze

narrate   *v.*   tell (a story), relate, recount, describe, reveal, make known, state, recite

narrow   *a.*   1. thin, not wide/broad, slender, contracted, restricted, limited, cramped
2. prejudiced, biased, narrow-minded, small-minded, petty

nasty   *a.*   unpleasant, offensive, mean, ill-tempered, disagreeable, spiteful, vindictive, dirty, unclean, filthy, rotten, polluted, foul

native   *a.*   1. inborn, inherent
2. natural, uncivilized
   n.   inhabitant, indigenous animal/plant/person

natural   *a.*   1. inborn, inherent, native
2. simple, unaffected, unadorned, usual, normal, lifelike, realistic, unpretentious, unforced

nature   *n.*   1. creation, the universe
2. quality, characteristic, manner, kind, sort
3. personality, disposition, character, instinct

naughty   *a.*   mischievous, misbehaved, badly-behaved, bad, ill-behaved, troublesome, disobedient, willful, wicked

navigate   *v.*   direct course, cruise, sail, steer, pilot

near   *adv.*   near by, close, nigh, at/to a short distance, neighboring
   a.   closely related/connected

nearly   *adv.*   almost, all but, closely

neat   *a.*   1. tidy, clean, orderly, trim, smart, well-groomed
2. adept, deft, adroit
3. pure, unadulterated, unmixed

necessary   *a.*   needful, essential, required, wanted, needed, indispensable

need   *v.*   want, require
   n.   want, lack, poverty, necessity, distress, hardship

needy   *a.*   in need/want/poverty/ distress, poor, destitute

negative   *a.*   not positive, contrary, opposite, difficult
   v.   refuse, forbid, disallow, oppose
   n.   photographic film/plate
in the negative: *no, not*
He replied in the **negative,** *"No, certainly not."*

neglect   *n.*   lack of care, carelessness, indifference, disregard
   v.   not care for/maintain/look after, miss, omit, ignore, fail, forget

neglectful	*a.*	careless, thoughtless, indifferent, remiss, negligent, inattentive
negotiate	*v.*	1. bargain, haggle, transact, make/arrange terms
		2. exchange, transfer, pass over/through
neighborhood	*n.*	vicinity, locality, district, area
nerve	*n.*	courage, pluck, daring, resolution, boldness
nervous	*a.*	nervy, fearful, timid, apprehensive, afraid, uneasy, tense, jumpy, shaky, jittery
net	*n.*	1. netting, mesh, grid, network, web
		2. snare, trap
	v.	snare, enmesh, trap, catch, capture
	a.	not gross, after deductions, real, actual
neutral	*a.*	neither for nor against, impartial, unbiased, without prejudice
new	*a.*	1. previously/hitherto unknown, unfamiliar, strange, different, novel, original
		2. recent, latest, fresh, unused
news	*n.*	information, tidings, bulletin, message, report
next	*a.*	nearest, adjacent, succeeding, following, after
nice	*a.*	1. pleasant, favorable, good, delicious, agreeable, friendly, lovely, charming, delightful, fine, delicate
		2. exact, precise, accurate
nil	*n.*	nothing, nought, zero
nimble	*a.*	quick, brisk, sprightly, spry, agile, lively, alive, active, alert, quick-witted

nip	*v.*	bite, pinch, squeeze
noble	*a.*	worthy, great, distinguished, honorable, eminent, celebrated, illustrious, lordly, dignified, majestic, brave, gallant, dashing
	n.	lord, peer, aristocrat, nobleman
nobody	*pron.*	no one/person
	n.	person of no importance/consequence
noise	*n.*	din, clamor, tumult, row, clatter, sound, discord, disharmony
none	*pron.*	no one, nobody, nothing
	a.	not one, not any
nonsense	*n.*	silliness, folly, absurdity, foolishness, idiocy, drivel, rubbish
normal	*a.*	usual, ordinary, regular, customary, habitual, general, standard, accepted, natural
notable	*a.*	great, famous, renowned, distinguished, noted, eminent, celebrated, illustrious, outstanding, remarkable, momentous, well-known
note	*n.*	1. fame, renown, greatness, eminence
		2. letter, message, communication
		3. jotting, memorandum, record, reminder
		4. musical sound
	v.	observe, notice, acknowledge
notice	*v.*	see, observe, note, attend, regard
	n.	1. warning, advice, announcement, proclamation, bulletin
		2. poster, circular, advertisement
notify	*v.*	inform, advise, tell

notion	*n.*	idea, fancy, whim, thought, impression, opinion, scheme, plan
nought	*n.*	nothing, nil, zero
nourish	*v.*	feed, sustain, care for, succor, nurture, support
novel	*a.*	new, original, fresh, different, unusual
	n.	story, tale, work of fiction
novice	*n.*	learner, beginner, initiate, starter, greenhorn, tyro
nude	*a.*	naked, bare, without clothes, unclothed, undressed, uncovered, exposed, bald
nudge	*v.*	push, poke, tap

nuisance	*n.*	pest, annoyance, offence, injury, bother, trouble, offensive/irritating/vexatious/troublesome/bothersome/annoying person
numb	*a.*	without feeling/sensation/sensibility, insensate, unfeeling, insensitive, dulled, deadened, paralyzed
number	*n.*	1. quantity, amount, sum 2. figure, digit
	v.	count, total, reckon, compute
numerous	*a.*	many, a lot of, various, abundant
nutritious	*a.*	nourishing, wholesome, feeding, strengthening

O o

oaf	n.	lout, dolt, blockhead, fool, idiot, buffoon, clown
oath	n.	1. solemn promise, pledge, vow 2. swear word, obscenity, profanity, blasphemy
obedient	a.	yielding, submissive, disciplined, dutiful, orderly, law-abiding, observant, compliant
obey	v.	yield/submit to, agree/comply with, observe
object	n.	1. thing, article, item 2. aim, intention, intent, ambition, purpose, hope, goal, target
object	v.	disapprove, protest, oppose, disagree, argue
obligation	n.	duty, promise, bond, task, responsibility
oblige	v.	1. help, aid, assist, favor, accommodate 2. make, force, require, expect, compel
obscure	a.	1. dark, dim, gloomy, misty, cloudy, hazy, nebulous, overshadowed 2. unknown, little-known, hidden, concealed, doubtful, dubious, indefinite, ambiguous
observant	a.	1. attentive, watchful, vigilant, alert, careful, cautious 2. obedient, submissive, compliant
observe	v.	1. look at, regard, notice, see, behold, watch, detect, examine 2. remark, comment, give an opinion 3. obey, submit to, comply with, pay regard to
obstacle	n.	hindrance, handicap, obstruction, bar, barrier, blockage, stoppage, impediment
obstinate	a.	stubborn, obdurate, unyielding, adamant, headstrong, determined, persistent
obstruct	v.	oppose, hinder, handicap, hamper, bar, block, stop, impede, retard
obtain	v.	get, take, secure, procure, acquire, earn, win
obvious	a.	clear, plain, easily seen, unmistakable, apparent, evident
occasion	n.	1. happening, occurrence, event, incident, episode, affair, circumstance, situation 2. reason, cause, need
	v.	cause, start, initiate, originate
occasional	a.	infrequent, uncommon, irregular, rare
occupation	n.	1. work, job, employment, business, trade, profession, vocation, calling, career 2. possession, ownership, residence, tenancy
occupy	v.	take up possession of, live/reside/dwell in, inhabit, possess, own
occur	v.	happen, take place, befall
occurrence	n.	happening, event, affair, incident, episode, experience

odd — *a.* 1. strange, unusual, peculiar, queer, abnormal, awkward, absurd, weird, eerie
2. not even, uneven, irregular, not uniform
3. not divisible by two

odious — *a.* nasty, unpleasant, distasteful, loathsome, obnoxious, disagreeable, displeasing, repulsive, offensive

odor — *n.* smell, scent, perfume, fragrance, aroma

offence — *n.* wrong, error, fault, crime, unlawful/illegal act/action, misdemeanor

offend — *v.* displease, hurt, harm, sin, insult, snub, vex, anger

offensive — *a.* disagreeable, unpleasant, displeasing, nasty, odious, distasteful, obnoxious, objectionable, putrid, foul

offer — *v.* proffer, hold out, make available, present, give, volunteer, suggest
n. gift, offering, present, sacrifice

office — *n.* 1. study, business headquarters
2. official post/position, duty

officer — *n.* commander, leader, official, representative, agent

official — *n.* officer, representative, agent
a. authorized, appointed, public

old — *a.* 1. olden, ancient, antiquated, old-fashioned, antique, aged, elderly
2. worn, decayed, neglected, unwanted

omit — *v.* leave out/undone, exclude, overlook, neglect, evade, disregard, fail, miss

once — *adv.* on one/a certain occasion, for/at one time

only — *a.* alone, lone, one, sole, single
adv. solely, singly, merely, but, just, exclusively, nothing more
conj. but then, were it not, besides

onward — *adv.* onwards, forward, forwards, to the front, in advance

open — *a.* 1. unshut, unhidden, uncovered, unclosed
2. sincere, frank, candid
v. 1. unclose, uncover, unfasten, unlock, disclose, reveal, release
2. begin, start, commence
open-eyed: *conscious, watchful, vigilant*
openhanded: *generous, liberal, benevolent*
open-minded: *fair, unbiased, unprejudiced, impartial*

opening — *n.* 1. gap, break, hole, aperture, entrance
2. opportunity, chance, occasion
a. starting, beginning, commencing, first, initial

operate — *v.* work, act, behave, manage, manipulate, drive

opinion — *n.* observation, belief, suggestion, comment

opponent — *n.* rival, competitor, antagonist, foe, enemy

opportune — *a.* accurately timed, well timed, just right, convenient

opportunity — *n.* good chance, opening, occasion

oppose — *v.* resist, react, be against, contradict, fight against

opposite — *a.* contrary, completely different, facing, face to face, opposed

pposition	*n.*	1. antagonism, hostility, hindrance, rivalry, defiance 2. group/party of opponents
ppress	*v.*	treat harshly/cruelly, overburden, crush, overwhelm, overpower, subjugate, subdue, suppress
pt	*v.*	pick, prefer, choose, select
ptimistic	*a.*	hopeful, sanguine
ption	*n.*	choice, preference, alternative
ral	*a.*	verbal, spoken, voiced, unwritten
rder	*n.*	1. instruction, demand, command, rule, regulation 2. request 3. way, method, technique 4. neatness, tidiness 5. rank, grade, class, category, arrangement, sequence
rderly	*a.*	1. ordered, methodical, well arranged/regulated, systematic, neat, tidy 2. well-behaved, well-conducted, disciplined, obedient, not unruly
ordinary	*a.*	common, commonplace, mediocre, usual, plain, homely, normal, regular, customary, habitual
organization	*n.*	1. system, method/way of operating, operation, arrangement 2. business, firm, company, society, establishment
origin	*n.*	source, beginning, start, cause
originate	*v.*	invent, devise, begin, start, cause
ornament	*n.*	decoration, adornment
outbreak	*n.*	1. outburst, eruption 2. rebellion, revolt, uprising
outfit	*n.*	set, collection, apparatus, equipment
outing	*n.*	trip, excursion, tour, expedition
outlaw	*n.*	robber, bandit, brigand, desperado, fugitive, renegade, criminal
outlet	*n.*	way out, egress, exit
outrageous	*a.*	dreadful, terrible, shocking, inexcusable, atrocious, awful, offensive, obnoxious
outside	*adv.*	outward, outwards, without
	a.	external, on the outside
outstanding	*a.*	superior, excellent, exceptional, famous, celebrated, notable, well-known, prominent
outward	*adv.*	outwards, outside
	a.	1. external, on the outside 2. on the surface, superficial
over	*prep.*	1. above, across 2. more than
	adv.	the opposite/reverse/other (side or face)
	a.	1. ended, finished, terminated, closed, completed, done 2. above, upper, covering
overcome	*v.*	beat, defeat, overpower, vanquish, overthrow, overwhelm, conquer, subdue
overflow	*v.*	flood, teem, be abundant/plentiful/in excess, proliferate
overlook	*v.*	1. pass by/over, ignore, disregard, tolerate, excuse, pardon, forgive 2. supervise, superintend, oversee
overpower	*v.*	overcome, beat, defeat, vanquish, overthrow, overwhelm, conquer, subdue

overthrow	*v.*	defeat, bring down, ruin, destroy	
overwhelm	*v.*	defeat, beat, conquer, vanquish, overpower, subdue, overcome, overthrow, swamp	

owe	*v.*	be in debt/a debtor
own	*v.*	1. hold, have, possess
		2. confess, admit, allow, grant, concede

P p

pace   *v.*   step, tread, walk, march, stride

         n.   1. stride, step
                2. speed, velocity, rate

pack   *n.*   1. set, stack
                2. package, parcel, bundle, case, knapsack, burden, load
                3. number, group (of hounds or wolves)

         v.   press/push/crowd together, compress, cram, fill, load

pad   *n.*   cushion, stuffing, block, stack

         v.   1. stuff, fill
                2. tramp, march

pagan   *n.*   heathen, idolater, barbarian

pain   *n.*   suffering, distress, anxiety, pang, ache, soreness, poignancy, twinge, agony
                take pains: *take trouble/care, make effort*

pair   *n.*   set of two, couple

         v.   arrange in couples, join, unite, mate

pale   *a.*   pallid, white, wan, ashen, grey, pasty, faded, faint, dim

paltry   *a.*   worthless, trifling, insignificant, petty, contemptible, despicable

pamper   *v.*   spoil, indulge, pet, coddle, humor

pan   *n.*   can, tin, dish, bowl, receptacle, container, vessel

pandemonium   *n.*   disorder, uproar, din, bedlam, tumult, chaos

panic   *n.*   fear, terror, fright, frenzy, alarm, haste, hurry, excitement, chaos

parade   *n.*   assembly, march, promenade, procession, display, show, exhibition

         v.   1. march, strut
                2. muster, assemble

paralyze   *v.*   make/render powerless/numb, disable, cripple, incapacitate

parched   *a.*   1. dry, arid, scorched, shriveled
                2. thirsty

pardon   *v.*   1. forgive, excuse, overlook, allow, absolve
                2. release, set free, discharge, acquit

part   *n.*   1. portion, fraction, bit, piece, section, share
                2. character, role

         v.   1. separate, divide, detach, split
                2. take leave

particular   *a.*   1. distinct, special, exclusive, individual
                2. careful, fastidious, choosy, selective

partner   *n.*   1. mate, associate, colleague, companion
                2. husband, wife, fiancé, fiancée, friend

party   *n.*   1. group, troop, band, faction
                2. feast, affair, function, ball, celebration

pass   *v.*   1. go/move/travel beyond, exceed
                2. transfer, deliver, hand over
                3. allow, sanction, approve

         n.   1. passage, gap, opening, path
                2. ticket, voucher, permit, passport

passage   *n.*   1. corridor, alley, lane, route, way, exit, entrance
                2. voyage, journey
                3. part, section, excerpt

passion   *n.*   emotion, fervor, devotion, ardor, excitement, fire

paste   *n.*   gum, glue, adhesive, mucilage, cement, fixative

pastime   *n.*   sport, recreation, amusement, hobby, pursuit

patch   *v.*   cover, mend, repair, cobble, sew, darn
      n.   1. pad, piece, strip
          2. plot, allotment

path   *n.*   footpath, track, way, route, road, lane

patient   *a.*   persevering, enduring, uncomplaining, long-suffering, tolerant, calm
      n.   invalid, sick person

patrol   *v.*   watch, guard, police, protect

pattern   *n.*   1. example, model, sample, specimen
          2. design, decoration, figure, arrangement

pause   *n.*   rest, interval, gap, intermission, recess, stop, halt

pay   *v.*   1. discharge, requite, reward, award, remunerate, recompense, compensate
          2. suffer, endure
      n.   payment, wages, salary, earnings

peaceful   *a.*   quiet, calm, tranquil, serene, restful, placid

peak   *n.*   1. highest point, top, tip, crest, crown, summit, pinnacle (of a mountain)
          2. brim (of a cap)

peculiar   *a.*   1. unusual, uncommon, strange, not normal, odd, eccentric, curious, queer
          2. personal, particular

peer   *v.*   look, glance, stare, peep
      n.   1. equal, match
          2. nobleman, aristocrat
          3. member of the House of Lords

penalty   *n.*   punishment, fine, imposition

penetrate   *v.*   enter, pass into/through, pierce, perforate, puncture

pensive   *a.*   thoughtful, reflective, dreamy, melancholy

people   *n.*   persons, folk, personnel, individuals

perfect   *a.*   excellent, faultless, flawless, superb, grand, fine, glorious, ideal, wonderful, exemplary, absolute, entire, complete

perfect   *v.*   complete, improve

perform   *v.*   do, act, achieve, accomplish

perfume   *n.*   scent, fragrance, sweet smell/odor/aroma

perhaps   *adv.*   maybe, possibly, perchance

peril   *n.*   danger, jeopardy, risk, hazard, menace, pitfall, trap

perish   *v.*   1. die, expire
          2. decay, rot, putrefy, decompose, wither, fade

permanent   *a.*   lasting, enduring, constant, endless, abiding

permit   *v.*   allow, let, authorize, sanction

permit   *n.*   pass, passport, license

perpendicular   *a.*   upright, erect, vertical, straight up

perpetual   *a.*   ceaseless, unceasing, eternal, everlasting, endless

perplex	*v.*	baffle, mystify, confound, bewilder, puzzle, confuse
persecute	*v.*	torment, ill-use, ill-treat, molest, plague, annoy, abuse, oppress, victimize
persevere	*v.*	strive, persist, try, endeavor
persist	*v.*	persevere, strive, try, endeavor
person	*n.*	one, someone, individual, man, woman, human being, mortal
personal	*a.*	private, privy, own, individual
personnel	*n.*	employees, staff
persuade	*v.*	sway, urge, compel, coax, entice, influence, encourage, convince
pest	*n.*	1. nuisance. annoyance, plague 2. harmful/destructive animal
pet	*n.*	favorite, darling, beloved, tamed animal
	v.	caress, fondle, cuddle, stroke
petty	*a.*	1. trivial, unimportant, insignificant, small 2. mean, small-minded, narrow-minded
pick	*v.*	1. choose, select, opt, prefer, elect 2. collect, gather, pluck, harvest
	n.	toothpick, pickaxe
picture	*n.*	illustration, sketch, drawing, painting, portrait, photograph
piece	*n.*	part, portion, fraction, bit, fragment, morsel, splinter, chip, lump
pierce	*v.*	penetrate, pass through/into, enter, stab, punch, perforate, puncture

pile	*n.*	1. heap, mound, collection, accumulation, mass, stack 2. post, stake 3 nap, surface (of fabric) *v.* heap, amass, collect, stack, assemble, load
pilot	*n.*	guide, conductor, steersman, helmsman, navigator, airman, aviator
pinch	*v.*	nip, squeeze, tweak
pine	*v.*	1. yearn, long, crave 2. waste away, fret, languish
pipe	*n.*	tube, stem, conduit, drain
pit	*n.*	1. hole, hollow, cavity, depression, indentation 2. mine, colliery
	v.	1. match, set 2. make pits/dents. indent
pitch	*v.*	1. hurl, fling, throw, cast, toss 2. move up and down, jolt, jump, shake 3. erect tents, encamp
	n.	1. tar, bitumen, asphalt 2. ground, spot, position 3. steepness, inclination
pitiful	*a.*	pathetic, sorrowful, sad, miserable, wretched, sorry
pity	*n.*	sympathy, compassion, mercy, consideration, grief, sorrow
place	*n.*	1. spot, locality, region, site, position 2. job, employment, office
	v.	1. put, position, set, lay, fix, locate, arrange 2. recognize, remember
plague	*v.*	bother, trouble, disturb, worry, pester, annoy, irritate, vex, tease, torment, tantalize
	n.	pestilence, epidemic

plain   *a.*   1. simple, straightforward, blunt, homely, homespun, unsophisticated, not decorated
                 2. clear, visible, easily seen/understood, obvious, distinct, unmistakable
                 3. level, even
      n.   prairie, steppe, plateau

plan   *n.*   1. map, chart, diagram, design
                 2. scheme, notion, idea, plot, motive, proposal, project, program, course, arrangement

plant   *v.*   1. sow, implant, set
                 2. put, place, position, deposit
      n.   1. herb, tree, shrub, weed
                 2. swindle, frame up, hoax
                 3. equipment, machinery, factory, mill
                 plants: *vegetation, plant-life, flora*

play   *n.*   1. performance, drama, act, production, theatricals
                 2. game, sport, amusement, entertainment
      v.   1. game, jest, frolic, frisk
                 2. act, perform

plead   *v.*   beg, beseech, entreat, implore, pray

pleasant   *a.*   pleasing, agreeable, delightful, cheerful, likeable, lovely, enjoyable, satisfying

please   *v.*   gladden, delight, cheer, satisfy, suit, thrill

plentiful   *a.*   abundant, sufficient, ample, generous, copious

plot   *n.*   1. plan, scheme, conspiracy, design
                 2. thread, theme (of a story or a play)
                 3. allotment, piece of ground, lot, patch

pluck   *v.*   gather, pick, snatch, grab, pull/take away, remove, harvest
      n.   bravery, courage, daring, spirit

plump   *a.*   fat, stout, chubby, obese, rotund

plunder   *v.*   ravage, sack, despoil, maraud, loot, rob, steal
      n.   loot, spoil, stolen goods

plunge   *v.*   1. dive, dip, immerse, submerge
                 2. thrust, push, force, drive

point   *n.*   1. tip, end
                 2. aim, purpose, object
                 3. place, position, location
                 4. headland, bluff, cape
      v.   aim, direct, level, line up

poke   *v.*   prod, jab, push, thrust, nudge

polish   *v.*   make smooth/shiny/glossy/lustrous, buff, burnish, rub
      n.   1. brightness, gloss, shine
                 2. courtesy, politeness, refinement

polite   *a.*   courteous, civil, well-mannered, mannerly, refined, gracious

poor   *a.*   1. impoverished, needy, in want/poverty, destitute
                 2. barren, infertile
                 3. inferior, mediocre, indifferent, miserable

popular   *a.*   favorite, well-liked

population   *n.*   people, inhabitants, citizens

portable   *a.*   movable, transportable, mobile

portion   *n.*   part, fraction, section, bit, piece, fragment, segment, share

position	*n.*	1. place, location, spot, site, point
		2. job, employment, situation, office, rank, post, status, station
		3. posture, attitude
positive	*a.*	certain, sure, definite, confident, assured, absolute
possess	*v.*	own, hold, have, keep, occupy
possibly	*adv.*	perhaps, maybe, perchance
post	*n.*	1. job, employment, situation, position, office, station
		2. place, location, spot
		3. stake, pole, beam, upright, support
		4. mail, letters, correspondence
poster	*n.*	notice, placard, display, advertisement, bill
postpone	*v.*	put/carry forward, put off, defer, delay
pot	*n.*	jar, vessel, container, pan, bowl, dish, basin
	v.	plant/preserve in pots
poverty	*n.*	need, want, shortage, impoverishment, scarcity, destitution
power	*n.*	1. ability, action, influence, control, mastery, authority
		2. effort, strength, might, energy, force, vigor
practicable	*a.*	workable, usable, useful, operational, effective
practical	*a.*	skilled, skilful, efficient
practice	*n.*	1. exercise, drill, training
		2. habit, custom, manner, method, procedure
praise	*v.*	1. applaud, commend, speak well of, approve, compliment
		2. worship, extol, glorify

preceding	*a.*	previous, prior, former, earlier, recent, preliminary, preparatory
precious	*a.*	costly, expensive, valuable, priceless, prized, treasured, cherished, much-loved, esteemed, admired
precise	*a.*	exact, accurate, fine, concise, specific, correct
predicament	*n.*	difficulty, plight, dilemma,
prefer	*v.*	1. like/want/desire/fancy more, choose, pick, select, favor
		2. promote
prejudice	*n.*	bias, partiality, unfairness, intolerance
preliminary	*a.*	introductory, opening, preparatory, preceding
prepare	*v.*	arrange, plan, organize, provide, take precautions, make/get ready
preposterous	*a.*	ridiculous, absurd, mad, nonsensical, silly, crazy, stupid, foolish, fantastic
presence	*n.*	attendance, existence, appearance
present	*a.*	here, existing, in person
	n.	gift, offer, donation, award
		at present: *now, nowad*ays *at this time/the moment*
present	*v.*	1. bestow, donate, give, offer
		2. introduce, announce, display, exhibit
presently	*adv.*	shortly, soon, before long, directly
preserve	*n.*	1. jam, jelly, confection, pickles, conserve
		2. sanctuary
	v.	protect, guard, maintain, shelter, keep safe, conserve

press   *v.*   1. push, squeeze, crush, compress, embrace
2. iron, smooth
3. urge, compel, drive, persuade, encourage

       n.   1. printing machine/press, journalism
2. mob, crowd

press on: *hurry, hasten, rush, dash*

pressing   *a.*   urgent, demanding, immediate, important

pressure   *n.*   force, effort, power, strength, stress, strain, tension

presume   *v.*   1. suppose, assume, take for granted, conclude, believe
2. take the liberty to/of

pretty   *a.*   pleasing, nice, delicate, dainty, attractive, handsome, beautiful, lovely

prevent   *v.*   avoid, preclude, stop, check, halt, arrest, prohibit, hinder, obstruct

previous   *a.*   preceding, prior, former, earlier, recent

price   *n.*   cost, charge, value, rate, expense

priceless   *a.*   very valuable/costly/expensive, invaluable, beyond price, precious, irreplaceable

prime   *a.*   1. first, primary, chief, main, principal
2. first-rate, perfect, superb, excellent, splendid

       n.   beginning/earlier part/dawn of life, youth, fullness of health, vigor

principal   *a.*   chief, main, head, leading, foremost, most important

       n.   chief, leader, head, director

principle   *n.*   rule, law, regulation, belief, truth, conviction

prison   *n.*   jail, penitentiary, reformatory, cell, dungeon

prisoner   *n.*   captive, convict, accused

private   *a.*   1. personal, privy, individual
2. secret, confidential
3. remote, isolated, secluded

prize   *v.*   1. value, esteem, treasure, cherish
2. force/pry (open/apart)

       n.   reward, gift, award, trophy, honor

probable   *a.*   likely, possible, almost/nearly certain/sure

problem   *n.*   1. puzzle, riddle, question, exercise
2. difficulty, burden, worry, trouble, hindrance

procedure   *n.*   method, way, process, plan, technique, arrangement, approach, action, movement

proceed   *v.*   1. begin, commence, start
2. move/travel forward, advance, continue
3. act, behave

proclaim   *v.*   announce, declare, publish

produce   *v.*   1. create, make, manufacture
2. yield, give, bring forth

product   *n.*   1. produce, goods, item, article
2. result, consequence

profession   *n.*   1. job, employment, trade, business, occupation, calling, vocation, career
2. declaration, admission, proclamation

profit   *n.*   gain, return, proceeds, benefit, advantage

program   *n.*   list, plan, scheme, schedule, catalog

progress   *v.*   move/travel forward, advance, continue, proceed, improve, grow, develop

prohibit	*v.*	forbid, disallow, ban, bar, stop, deny, prevent
project	*n.*	plan, scheme, design, task, undertaking, ventur
project	*v.*	1. stick/jut out, protrude, extend 2. throw, thrust, fling, hurl, shoot, eject
prolong	*v.*	lengthen, make longer, extend, increase, expand, stretch, continue
prominent	*a.*	1. famous, celebrated, notable, eminent, well-known 2. outstanding, clearly/ plainly seen
promise	*n.*	intention, assurance, guarantee, pledge, agreement, vow
promising	*a.*	encouraging, hopeful, optimistic
prompt	*a.*	immediate, without delay, quick, fast, rapid, speedy, swift, ready, punctual
	v.	encourage, help, assist, inspire
pronounce	*v.*	utter, articulate, speak distinctly/clearly
propel	*v.*	push/send/force forward, thrust, drive, impel
proper	*a.*	correct, just, right, exact, appropriate, suitable, becoming, fitting, seemly, demure
property	*n.*	1. possessions, belongings, land, wealth, assets 2. characteristic, quality, nature
propose	*v.*	offer, suggest, submit, recommend, put forward
prosper	*v.*	succeed, thrive, grow, flourish, do well, become wealthy
protect	*v.*	shield, shelter, defend, guard, keep safe, preserve
protest	*v.*	object, oppose, grumble, complain, disagree
proud	*a.*	1. vain, conceited, disdainful, haughty, boastful, self-satisfied, arrogant 2. dignified, stately, noble
prove	*v.*	1. find proof/evidence of/for, confirm, verify, demonstrate, show 2. check, test, examine
proverb	*n.*	maxim, adage, saying, byword
provide	*v.*	supply, give, furnish, arrange, prepare, equip, provision, produce
provisions	*n.*	supplies, foodstuffs, victuals
prowl	*v.*	steal about, lurk, roam, wander
prudent	*a.*	wise, sagacious, careful, cautious, thrifty, wary, far seeing, far sighted
public	*n.*	people, populace, inhabitants, community, society
publish	*v.*	make known, reveal, announce, proclaim, broadcast
pull	*v.*	draw, tug, tow, yank, snatch, haul, drag, attract
punch	*v.*	1. strike, thump, poke, pummel, hit 2. pierce, perforate, puncture
punish	*v.*	chastise, correct, discipline, penalize, take revenge
pupil	*n.*	learner, scholar, student
purchase	*v.*	buy, acquire, gain
pure	*a.*	1. clean, unadulterated, unmixed, untainted, spotless, immaculate, genuine 2. innocent, blameless, chaste, stainless, unblemished, perfect, unsullied, virtuous

purify	*v.*	1. make pure, clean, cleanse, refine, filter
		2. free from sin, absolve
purpose	*n.*	meaning, intention, object, aim, plan, ambition
pursue	*v.*	hunt, chase, follow, seek, track

push	*v.*	thrust, shove, press, prod, poke, nudge
puzzle	*n.*	problem, riddle, poser, maze
	v.	perplex, baffle, mystify, bewilder, confuse, confound

Q q

quack *n.* 1. duck's cry, harsh voice, discordant sound

2. humbug, impostor, charlatan, mountebank, pretender, deceiver

v. talk loudly and foolishly, speak boastfully

quack doctor: *vendor/ prescriber of inferior medicines/remedies*

quagmire *n.* bog, marsh, morass, mire, swamp, slough, fen

quake *v.* shake, shiver, tremble, shudder, quiver, quaver, rock, vibrate, throb

qualified *a.* trained, able, competent, capable, experienced, fit, suitable

qualify *v.* 1. train, prepare, make competent/capable/fit/ suitable, give/obtain qualification/diploma/ certificate/degree

2. modify, make limitations/reservations, moderate, mitigate, alter, improve, change, make less absolute, amend

quality *n.* 1. kind, character, grade, standard, class, group, category, degree, badness/goodness of

2. characteristic, attribute, trait, faculty, accomplishment, skill, talent

qualm *n.* 1. doubt, uneasiness, disquiet, misgiving, conscience, scruple

2. momentary/touch of faintness/sickness/nausea

quantity *n.* amount, number, size, measure, mass, weight, volume, estimate, sum, total, part, portion, proportion, extent

quarrel *v.* dispute/differ/disagree/ argue/contend angrily, wrangle, altercate, squabble, row, fall out, bicker, find fault, take exception

quarry *n.* hunted/pursued/chased animal/person, prey, game, intended victim

quarters *n.* accommodation, lodgings, abode, residence, billet, barracks, cabin

quash *v.* crush, subdue, suppress, quell, annul, make void, invalidate, put/make an end to, terminate, ban, bar, disallow, oppose, reject

queer *a.* 1. peculiar, odd, strange, not ordinary/normal, abnormal, unusual, bizarre, eccentric, suspect, suspicious, shady, questionable, doubtful, dubious

2. out of sorts, unwell, ill, sick, indisposed, giddy, faint, drunk

quell *v.* crush, subdue, suppress, overcome, put down, force to/make submit

quench *v.* 1. extinguish, put out, destroy

2. end, satisfy, slake (thirst), cool (with water)

query *v.* question, inquire, check, investigate

quest *n.* search, inquiry, hunt, chase, pursuit, investigation

question	*v.*	ask questions about, query, inquire, seek information from, interrogate, examine, oppose, raise objection to, doubt, be dubious about, dispute
questionable	*a.*	doubtful, in doubt, dubious, debatable, disputable, in dispute, unsure, uncertain, possibly untrue, not consistent, inconsistent
quick	*a.*	1. quick-moving, rapid, fast, speedy, swift, fleet, brisk, sudden, immediate, instantaneous
		2. agile, nimble, spry, active, lively, alive, energetic, vigorous, alert, quick-witted, keen, eager
		3. sharp, short, snappy, abrupt, curt, brusque, hasty, impatient, impetuous, harsh, irritable, irascible
quiet	*a.*	1. silent, without noise, noiseless, subdued, hushed, inaudible
		2. still, restful, at rest, tranquil, peaceful, serene, demure, reposed, undisturbed, docile, placid, unmotivated, inactive, unobtrusive
		She wore a **quiet** dress.

quit	*v.*	1. leave, go away/depart/ retire from, go out of, vacate, desert
		2. forsake, let go, give up, resign, abandon, relinquish, surrender
		3. stop, cease, discontinue
		quitter: *deserter, coward, poltroon, shirker, slacker*
quite	*adv.*	1. completely, entirely, fully, wholly, altogether, to the fullest/utmost extent, positively, definitely, absolutely, truly, really
		2. rather, to some extent, fairly, more or less
quiver	*v.*	tremble, shake, shiver, shudder, quake, quaver, twitch, vibrate, throb, rock
	n.	sheath, holder, case, container
		The archer keeps his arrows in a **quiver.**
quiz	*n.*	set of questions/queries/ problems/puzzles/riddles, questionnaire, test, examination, interrogation
quotation	*n.*	1. words/passage quoted, exact copy/repeat of the words, quote, extract, excerpt, selection
		2. price quoted/given/ named/stated

R r

ace

v. flow, run, sprint, dash, hurry, hasten, speed

n. 1. flow, current, stream
2. contest, competition, match
3. family, tribe, clan, stock people, nation

ack

n. frame, framework, shelves

v. pain, hurt, torment, torture, agonize

acket

n. 1. uproar, din, row, noise, bedlam, disturbance, tumult, hubbub, commotion
2. bat, racquet
3. fraud, swindle

adiate

v. scatter, spread, shed, broadcast, give/send off/out, transmit, emit

age

n. anger, annoyance, fury, frenzy, wrath, passion

agged

a. torn, tattered, threadbare, shabby

aid

v. attack, invade, plunder, loot, pillage, ravage

ail

n. beam, bar, barrier, fence

v. scold, threaten, abuse

aise

v. 1. erect, elevate, lift, hoist
2. increase, advance
3. grow, cultivate, rear, breed
4. bring up, educate
5. collect, gather, levy (taxes, soldiers, etc.)
6. stir up, agitate, rouse
raise Cain: *stir up trouble, make a fuss/disturbance*

ramble

v. 1. stroll, roam, wander, straggle, walk
2. digress, wander away, stray from the subject

range

n. 1. extent, scope, limit, spread
2. line, row, rank

v. roam, rove, wander, stroll, straggle

rank

n. 1. line, row, range, queue
2. class, category, quality, gràde, order, position, status

a. 1. luxuriant, coarse, gross, choked
2. rotting, decaying, foul-smelling, indecent, corrupt
3. unmistakable, flagrant, virulent

ransack

v. search thoroughly, loot, plunder, pillage, sack

rap

n. 1. tap, knock, bump, thump, whack, slap, blow, bang
2. jot, bit, little/least bit

rapid

a. quick, fast, swift, speedy

rare

a. uncommon, unusual, scarce, infrequent, extraordinary, peculiar, odd

rascal

n. rogue, scamp, imp, ˌvagabond, scoundrel, ruffian, villain, culprit

rash

a. reckless, wild, headstrong, impetuous, foolhardy, hasty, careless, thoughtless

rate

n. 1. price, cost, charge, value, amount
2. estimate, assessment, appraisal
3. velocity, speed, swiftness, pace

rather

adv. 1. sooner, preferably, more truly, for choice
2. to some extent, slightly, somewhat

rattle	*n.*	noise, sound, din, clatter, chatter, babble
	v.	confuse, fluster, frighten, make nervous/apprehensive
rave	*v.*	1. shout/yell/talk wildly/ madly/furiously, rage, roar, rant, fume
		2. be excited/thrilled, enthuse
ravenous	*a.*	very hungry/greedy, starving, famished, voracious
raw	*a.*	1. fresh, uncooked, unprepared
		2. untrained, inexperienced
		3. sore, sensitive
		4. very cold, bitter, bleak, chilly
ready	*a.*	1. willing, prepared, available, handy
		2. prompt, quick, speedy, swift, immediate
real	*a.*	actual, authentic, true, genuine, honest
realize	*v.*	1. understand, comprehend, appreciate, recognize, know, be aware
		2. make realistic
		3. convert, amass, fetch
		The sale **realized** $146.95.
rear	*a.*	back, hindmost, rearmost
	n.	end, back, background
	v.	1. bring up, train, educate
		2. raise, breed
		3. build, erect, raise lip
reason	*n.*	1. cause, purpose, motive,
		2. aim mind, intelligence, intellect, judgement
	v.	think, judge, conclude
reasonable	*a.*	proper, right, just, sensible, fair, moderate
rebel	*v.*	revolt, mutiny, disobey
rebel	*n.*	revolutionary, traitor, insurgent, mutineer

recall	*v.*	1. remember, recollect
		2. call/summon back
		3. take/bring back, withdraw
receive	*v.*	take, accept, gain, obtain, acquire, get
recent	*a.*	1. latest, new, modern
		2. preceding, foregoing, previous
recite	*v.*	repeat, relate, retell, narrate deliver, quote
reckless	*a.*	rash, wild, headstrong, impetuous, foolhardy, hasty, careless, thoughtless, harum-scarum
reckon	*v.*	count, calculate, estimate, judge, compute
recline	*v.*	rest, repose, lie, loll, lean back, sprawl
recognize	*v.*	1. remember, recollect, recall, know, identify
		2. admit, accept, comprehend, understand, appreciate, see, know, realize
recollect	*v.*	recall, remember, call to mind
recommend	*v.*	advise, suggest, commend, approve of, make acceptable
record	*n.*	1. written account, note, list inventory, report, memorandum, entry
		2. best/finest achievement/result
		3. disc, tape, cassette
recover	*v.*	1. get/bring/fetch/win back, regain, restore, reclaim
		2. become/get well/better, return/restore to health, improve, revive, recuperate
recreation	*n.*	leisure, amusement, game, sport, pursuit, hobby, interest, pastime

reduce	*v.*	1. lessen, decrease, shrink, contract, diminish, bring down 2. convert, change 3. conquer, subdue 4. weaken, impoverish
reflect	*v.*	1. consider, think over, meditate, ponder, study 2. rebound, return, mirror, reproduce
reform	*v.*	1. rearrange, change, alter 2. improve, better, correct, amend
refresh	*v.*	freshen, renew, enliven, restore, revive, strengthen, stimulate
refuge	*n.*	place of safety, shelter, sanctuary, haven, retreat, protection
refuse	*v.*	decline, reject, turn down, put aside
refuse	*n.*	rubbish, waste, litter, garbage
regain	*v.*	get/bring/fetch/win back, recover, retrieve
regard	*v.*	look at, observe, view, behold
	n.	esteem, admiration, approval
region	*n.*	area, section, part, locality, district, territory, land, country
register	*n.*	record, official list, roll, inventory
regret	*v.*	be sorry, bewail, repent, apologize, mourn, grieve, lament
regular	*a.*	1. constant, permanent 2. correct, proper, normal, customary, usual, standard 3. methodical
rehearse	*v.*	perfect, practice, repeat
reject	*v.*	refuse, decline, return, discard, throw out, eliminate
relate	*v.*	1. tell, say, state, narrate, recount, describe 2. belong, connect, associate
relax	*v.*	1. abate, become less severe/powerful, reduce, lessen, release, slacken 2. take ease/comfort, rest
release	*v.*	free, liberate, set free/loose, relax, discharge, let go, unfasten
reliable	*a.*	dependable, trustworthy, loyal, faithful, sure, safe, certain, accurate
relieve	*v.*	1. help, assist, aid, soothe, ease, alleviate, palliate, comfort 2. take over from, replace
reluctant	*a.*	unwilling, not willing/keen/anxious, loath, hesitant
rely	*v.*	depend, trust, count
remain	*v.*	1. stay, rest, linger, loiter, tarry 2. survive, endure, last
remark	*v.*	1. say, comment, mention 2. observe, notice, note
remarkable	*a.*	unusual, uncommon, noteworthy, amazing, extraordinary, marvelous, wonderful
remedy	*v.*	cure, heal, restore, repair, relieve
	n.	cure, restorative, prescription, treatment
remember	*v.*	1. recall, recollect, bring to mind 2. think of/about, mention 3. reward, tip
remind	*v.*	prompt, jog memory

remote	*a.*	distant, far off/away, isolated, lonely, secluded
remove	*v.*	1. take from/away, sequester, displace, detach 2. transfer, convey, carry 3. dismiss, sack
repair	*v.*	1. remedy, restore, mend, patch, cobble, overhaul, correct 2. go, depart, travel
repay	*v.*	reward, pay back, return, refund
repeat	*v.*	say/do again, copy, reproduce, retell, recite, recount
replace	*v.*	1. put back, return, restore 2. substitute, exchange
reply	*v.*	answer, retort, respond, echo
report	*n.*	1. statement, account, comment, message, story, rumor, news, advice, intelligence, declaration, announcement, disclosure 2. explosion, bang, noise
reproduce	*v.*	1. repeat, copy, duplicate, print, trace 2. breed, multiply
require	*v.*	1. want, need, desire, wish for 2. ask, request, solicit
rescue	*v.*	aid, help, free/remove/deliver from danger, save, recover
research	*n.*	study, inquiry, investigation
reserve	*v.*	store, keep, retain, save, withhold, set aside, book, arrange
reserved	*a.*	1. booked, saved, kept, set aside, retained 2. shy, modest, quiet, bashful, retiring
reside	*v.*	live, dwell, abide, lodge, inhabit, occupy
residence	*n.*	dwelling, home, house, quarters
resign	*v.*	leave, quit, give up, surrender, retire
resist	*v.*	withstand, oppose, defy, check, thwart
resolution	*n.*	1. resolve, intention, aim, decision, plan, scheme 2. determination, strength of purpose
resourceful	*a.*	ingenious, skilful, inventive, imaginative
respect	*n.*	esteem, appreciation, honor, regard, admiration
respectable	*a.*	worthy, honorable, decent, proper
responsible	*a.*	1. answerable, liable, accountable 2. dependable, reliable, trustworthy
restful	*a.*	relaxing, comfortable, easy, leisurely, quiet, placid, peaceful, tranquil, soothing
restless	*a.*	uneasy, unsettled, agitated, fidgety, disturbed, apprehensive
restore	*v.*	1. replace, return, give/put/pay/bring back, refund, repay 2. repair, mend 3. heal, cure, revive, make well
restrain	*v.*	check, hold back, stop, hinder, restrict, control, prevent
restrict	*v.*	limit, confine, restrain, control, hold back
result	*n.*	answer, outcome, effect, consequence, product, conclusion

resume	v.	begin/commence/start again, go on, continue, proceed with	**riddle**	n.	problem, puzzle, secret, mystery
				v.	perforate, puncture
retire	v.	withdraw, retreat, depart, go away/back	**ridicule**	v.	mock, make fun of, laugh/jeer at, tease
retort	n.	reply, response, answer		n.	scorn, sarcasm, mockery, jeers
return	v.	1. put/give/bring back, restore, recover, replace	**ridiculous**	a.	absurd, silly, nonsensical, foolish, stupid, unreasonable, preposterous
		2. come/go/travel back, reappear	**right**	a.	correct, proper, just, true, fair, exact, appropriate, suitable, lawful
	n.	1. restoration, recovery			
		2. reappearance		n.	liberty, privilege
		3. repayment, refund			
		4. profit, gain, proceeds	**rigid**	a.	stiff, firm, unbending
reveal	v.	disclose, unveil, unmask, expose, show	**ring**	n.	circle, circlet, loop, band, enclosure
				v.	sound, tinkle, jingle, chime
reverse	v.	1. turn round/inside out	**ripe**	a.	full-grown, mature, ready, mellow, fully developed
		2. go/move/travel backwards			
		3. cancel, undo, alter	**rise**	v.	1. arise, get/stand up
	n.	1. opposite/other			2. ascend, climb, go upwards
		2. defeat, failure, loss			3. increase, swell, expand
					4. originate, begin
revise	v.	correct, alter, change, improve, amend		n.	hill, mound, slope, elevation
revive	v.	refresh, restore, renew			
revolt	v.	rebel, disobey, mutiny, desert	**risk**	n.	danger, peril, hazard, chance, dare
	n.	rebellion, mutiny, desertion	**rival**	n.	opponent, competitor, adversary, enemy
revolting	a.	horrible, hideous, disgusting, loathsome, offensive, very unpleasant, noxious, odious, repulsive	**road**	n.	highway, route, track, path, way, thoroughfare
			roam	v.	wander, ramble, stroll, walk, stray, straggle
revolve	v.	turn, spin, rotate, whirl, gyrate	**rob**	v.	steal, loot, plunder, maraud, pillage, raid, pilfer
reward	n.	payment, gift, prize, profit, bonus	**robber**	n.	bandit, brigand, ruffian, raider, pirate, footpad, highwayman, thief, burglar
ribald	a.	obscene, irreverent, scurrilous			
			robust	a.	strong, healthy, sturdy, hardy, vigorous, virile
rich	a.	1. wealthy, prosperous			
		2. abundant, rank, luxuriant, fertile, fruitful	**rock**	v.	sway, stagger, reel, wobble
		3. bright, gaudy, deep, vivid		n.	stone, pebble, boulder

rogue	*n.*	rascal, vagabond, scoundrel, ruffian, scapegrace, scamp, imp, villain	

roll　*v.*　1. turn over, rotate, revolve, wind, reel, spin
2. flatten, level, press

　　　n.　1. register, official list, catalog, inventory
2. bun, small loaf

romantic　*a.*　fanciful, imaginative, sentimental

root　*n.*　1. foundation, bottom, base
2. cause, reason, origin, beginning, source

rot　*v.*　decay, perish, putrefy, decompose, spoil

rotate　*v.*　turn, spin, revolve, roll, whirl

rough　*a.*　1. coarse, uneven, irregular
2. wild, stormy, disorderly
3. severe, harsh
4. uncouth, boorish, common, vulgar, rude, crude

round　*a.*　1. ball-shaped, spherical, globular
2. circle-shaped, ring-shaped, circular, smooth

rouse　*v.*　arouse, awaken, wake, wake up, stir up, alarm, startle, stimulate

rout　*v.*　defeat, beat, vanquish, conquer, put to flight

route　*n.*　way, course, road, path, track

routine　*a.*　orderly, systematic, customary, regular, general, usual

row　*n.*　1. quarrel, dispute, disagreement, altercation
2. noise, din, clatter, bedlam, uproar, tumult, disturbance, commotion

rub　*v.*　1. stroke, massage
2. smear, wipe, scratch, mark

rubbish　*n.*　waste, litter, junk, trash, debris, refuse, garbage, lumber

rude　*a.*　coarse, common, vulgar, boorish, uncouth, impolite, discourteous, rough

ruin　*v.*　wreck, destroy, spoil, damage

rumor　*n.*　news, gossip, hearsay, tattle, talk, tale

run　*v.*　1. move/travel fast/quickly/ swiftly, flow, race, career, sprint, spurt, dash, glide, dart, scamper, speed, rush
2. manage, direct, control

　　　n.　trip, journey, excursion

rural　*a.*　country, rustic, of the countryside, agricultural

rush　*v.*　move/travel quickly/swiftly, dash, stampede, charge, career, hasten, hurry, speed

ruthless　*a.*　without pity/mercy, harsh, pitiless, merciless, cruel, brutal

S s

sack	*v.*	1. dismiss (from job/employment), fire
		2. plunder, pillage, loot, ravage
	n.	large bag
sacred	*a.*	holy, consecrated, sanctified, hallowed, dedicated, sacrosanct, revered
sad	*a.*	unhappy, sorrowful, miserable, gloomy, dejected, downcast, depressed, dismal, woeful, melancholy, doleful, mournful, lugubrious
safe	*a.*	1. secure, protected, sheltered
		2. trustworthy, reliable, dependable
sample	*n.*	specimen, example, pattern, model, illustration
	v.	take/give samples, try, test
satisfactory	*a.*	suitable, adequate, acceptable, appropriate
satisfy	*v.*	please, content, suit, gratify
saturated	*a.*	soaked, drenched, sodden, soggy
saucy	*a.*	cheeky, impertinent, impudent, forward, bold, brazen, rude, flippant
savage	*a.*	1. wild, untamed, fierce, ferocious
		2. barbarous, uncivilized, cruel, brutal
		3. angry, enraged, furious, mad, violent
save	*v.*	1. rescue, deliver, liberate, set free
		2. safeguard, store, keep, gather, hoard, put by, preserve, collect
		3. economize, be sparing/careful/thrifty
	prep.	except, leaving out, omitting
say	*v.*	state, speak, utter, tell, declare, announce, express, assert
saying	*n.*	proverb, byword, maxim, adage
scamp	*n.*	rascal, scapegrace, rogue, imp, scallywag, scoundrel knave
	v.	skimp, dodge
scanty	*a.*	meager, skimpy, sparse, inadequate, insufficient, little, poor
scarce	*a.*	meager, rare, short, sparse, not plentiful, insufficient
scare	*v.*	frighten, alarm, startle, terrify
scatter	*v.*	1. strew, sprinkle, spread, sow, broadcast, distribute
		2. separate, disperse, break up
scene	*n.*	view, vista, sight, landscape, panorama
scent	*n.*	smell, odor, perfume, fragrance, aroma
scheme	*n.*	plan, design, plot, project, undertaking, venture
scoff	*v.*	mock, jeer, sneer, deride, gibe (jibe), taunt, ridicule
scold	*v.*	rebuke, reprimand, reprove, criticize, find fault with
scorn	*v.*	despise, spurn, disdain, be contemptuous, sneer, reject, condemn

scoundrel   *n.*   rogue, rascal, villain, scamp, scallywag, knave

scrap   *n.*   1. bit, piece, portion, remnant, morsel, shred, fragment
2. waste, rubbish, junk, refuse

       v.   1. discard, throw away
2. quarrel, fight, brawl

scratch   *v.*   tear, claw, mark, disfigure

scrawl   *v.*   scribble, write hastily/badly

scream   *v.*   cry/shout loudly, bawl, yell, shriek, screech, squeal, bellow

screen   *n.*   1. cover, protection, shelter, mask
2. partition, divider
3. sieve, net

search   *v.*   look for, seek, explore, probe, ransack

secret   *a.*   hidden, concealed, unknown, confidential, mysterious

section   *n.*   part, portion, fraction, piece, segment, sector, division, region

secure   *a.*   safe, fast, tight, firm, solid, stable

       v.   1. obtain, get, procure
2. fortify, make safe, enclose
3. fasten, tie up, moor

see   *v.*   1. look at, observe, perceive, regard, watch
2. know, understand, comprehend, follow, grasp

seize   *v.*   1. grab, grip, grasp, clutch, hold
2. capture, arrest, take
3. steal, rob, snatch, plunder, loot, carry off, annex

seldom   *adv.*   not often, rarely, infrequently, occasionally

select   *v.*   pick, choose, designate, indicate

sell   *v.*   vend, deal/trade in, market, retail, peddle

send   *v.*   dispatch, forward, transmit, propel, drive

senseless   *a.*   1. without sense, stupid, silly, foolish, nonsensical, ridiculous, pointless, absurd
2. insensible, unconscious

sensible   *a.*   1. intelligent, not foolish, wise, thoughtful, practical, astute, shrewd
2. conscious, aware, alert

separate   *a.*   divided, disconnected, distinct, unconnected, detached, apart, individual

serene   *a.*   calm, tranquil, composed, untroubled, undisturbed, peaceful, placid

serious   *a.*   1. grave, critical
2. solemn, sober, sombre, dignified, important
3. thoughtful, pensive, earnest, sincere

set   *v.*   1. place, put, plant, stand, sink
2. harden, solidify, become hard/solid

       n.   group, pack, kit, outfit

settle   *v.*   1. rest, alight, sink
2. pay
3. arrange, determine, decide

settle in: *colonize, inhabit*

sever   *v.*   cut, separate, divide

severe   *a.*   1. stern, strict, harsh, stiff
2. plain, simple, austere, unadorned
3. intense, violent

shabby	*a.*	1. threadbare, worn, poor, drab, ragged, dilapidated
		2. paltry, petty, mean, miserable, spiteful, unfair, unkind
shady	*a.*	1. shaded, shadowy, darkened, gloomy
		2. dishonest, crooked, suspicious
shake	*v.*	1. tremble, shiver, quake, quiver, shudder, wobble, vibrate, agitate
		2. wave, brandish, flourish
sham	*a.*	false, bogus, feigned, pretended, imitation, counterfeit
shame	*v.*	disgrace, dishonor, discredit, humiliate
shameless	*a.*	without shame, bold, brazen, forward, rude, vulgar, common, indecent, disgraceful
shape	*v.*	form, fashion, mold, construct, build
	n.	form, figure, outline, pattern, contour
share	*v.*	1. divide, allot, apportion, ration
		2. take part, participate
sharp	*a.*	1. keen, pointed, piercing, penetrating, cutting
		2. painful, stinging, bitter, pungent, biting, acid, severe, harsh
		3. quick-witted, alert, bright, smart, intelligent, clever, shrewd, astute, vigilant, wary, watchful
sheer	*a.*	1. abrupt, steep
		2. complete, absolute, utter
		3. transparent, thin
shelter	*n.*	shield, screen, protection, cover, refuge, harbor, sanctuary, haven

shield	*n.*	shelter, screen, cover, protection, guard
shift	*v.*	1. move/change/alter position
		2. manage, make do, carry on, survive, exist
shine	*v.*	give out/emit/radiate light, glow, glisten, gleam
	n.	brightness, luster, brilliance, gloss
shiver	*v.*	shake, tremble, quake, quiver, shudder
shock	*n.*	1. fright, alarm
		2. blow, collision, impact, jolt, shake
	v.	startle, frighten, alarm, dismay, appall, astound, astonish
short	*a.*	1. not long/lengthy/tall, small, brief, concise, laconic
		2. scanty, meager, lacking, insufficient, deficient, in need
		3. curt, terse, abrupt, sharp, quick, nasty, uncivil
shortage	*n.*	lack, inadequacy, insufficiency, deficiency
shout	*v.*	cry/call loudly, yell, bawl, bellow, scream
show	*v.*	1. display, reveal, exhibit, demonstrate, present
		2. explain, guide, instruct
shred	*n.*	scrap, fragment, bit, piece, flake, shaving, strip
	v.	tear, rip, fragment
shrewd	*a.*	wise, sagacious, discerning, astute, knowing, observant, alert, sharp, clever, cunning
shrill	*a.*	keen, piercing, penetrating, high-pitched, loud, sharp
shut	*a.*	1. not open, closed, fastened
		2. confined, enclosed, contained

shy   *a.*   timid, cautious, wary, reserved, reticent, modest, bashful

     v.   throw, toss, pitch, hurl

     shy away: *hang back, take fright*

sick   *a.*   ill, unwell, ailing, indisposed, unhealthy

sign   *n.*   signal, token, symbol, trace, mark, emblem, badge, indication, gesture

signal   *v.*   beckon, gesture, indicate, betoken, send a message

     n.   sign, symbol

     a.   noteworthy, worthwhile, memorable

significant   *a.*   important, notable, noteworthy, meaningful, prominent, expressive

silent   *a.*   quiet, without noise/sound, noiseless, soundless, still, hushed

silly   *a.*   foolish, stupid, absurd, daft, senseless, nonsensical, puerile, pointless, ridiculous, inane, simple-minded, simple-witted

simple   *a.*   1. not difficult, easy, elementary

     2. plain, unadorned, austere

     3. open, frank, candid, honest, straightforward, true, truthful

sincere   *a.*   honest, true, genuine, straightforward, not hypocritical, trustworthy

site   *n.*   location, situation, place, spot, position, ground

situation   *n.*   1. site, location, place, spot

     2. position, appointment, job, employment, office

     3. predicament, plight

skillful   *a.*   skilled, able, expert, clever, capable, competent, efficient, dexterous

slack   *a.*   1. loose, limp, flabby, flaccid

     2. lazy, slow, indolent, lax, negligent, indifferent, careless

slay   *v.*   kill, slaughter, massacre, destroy

sleek   *a.*   smooth, glossy, shiny, velvety, silky, lustrous

sleep   *v.*   slumber, repose, doze

slender   *a.*   1. slim, thin, narrow

     2. slight, scanty, meager, insufficient, inadequate

slight   *a.*   1. small, trifling, trivial, insignificant, unimportant

     2. slim, slender, thin, delicate

     v.   insult, ignore, disregard, neglect, snub

slim   *a.*   1. slender, thin, narrow

     2. delicate, fragile, slight, frail, weak

slip   *n.*   1. stumble, stagger, fall

     2. mistake, error, fault, blunder

     3. small piece/sheet of paper, note

sly   *a.*   crafty, cunning, artful, deceitful, underhanded, treacherous, stealthy

small   *a.*   little, tiny, slight, undersized, puny, paltry, insignificant, trivial, unimportant, trifling

smart   *a.*   1. clever, talented, bright, intelligent, sharp, alert, keen, shrewd

     2. neat, tidy, handsome, stylish, fashionable

     3. sharp, biting, stinging

smell   *n.*   scent, odor, fragrance, aroma, perfume, stink, stench

smooth	*a.*	1. even, flat, level, polished 2. calm, peaceful, tranquil, still, serene, placid	**sorrow**	*n.*	sadness, unhappiness, misery, grief, woe, suffering, distress, remorse, anxiety, heartache
snatch	*v.*	grab, grip, seize, grasp, take, clutch	**sorry**	*a.*	1. sorrowful, sad, grieved, regretful, remorseful, penitent 2. poor, miserable, unfortunate, wretched, pathetic, pitiful
sneer	*v.*	scorn, disdain, taunt, jeer, gibe (jibe), mock, belittle			
sob	*v.*	cry, weep, gulp	**sort**	*n.*	kind, type, group, grade, class, quality, nature
sober	*a.*	calm, sensible, grave, dignified, demure, temperate, not drunk/ inebriated/intoxicated	**sound**	*n.*	1. noise, din, clamor 2. channel, strait
				a.	1. wise, sensible, correct, right, reliable, intelligent, good 2. whole, complete, strong, healthy, hearty, sturdy, vigorous, stable, substantial
soft	*a.*	1. not hard/solid, yielding, weak, limp, pliable, flexible 2. gentle, tender, mild, kind, sympathetic 3. low, subdued			
			sour	*a.*	1. acid, vinegary, tart, bitter, sharp-tasting, nasty 2. bad-tempered, ill-tempered, surly, sullen
soggy	*a.*	saturated, soaked, drenched, sodden, wet, damp, moist			
solemn	*a.*	serious, grave, sober, sad, sorrowful, mournful, dignified	**source**	*n.*	origin, beginning
			souvenir	*n.*	memento, keepsake, reminder
solid	*a.*	1. not hollow/empty, firm, hard, rigid 2. sound, reliable, wise, dependable, stable, steady, steadfast, trustworthy, sensible	**space**	*n.*	1. room, accommodation 2. break, gap 3. infinity, beyond the Earth, the universe 4. period/interval (of time), spell, while
solitary	*a.*	1. lone, alone, single, only, sole 2. lonely, desolate, barren, deserted, isolated, secluded, remote	**spare**	*a.*	scanty, meager, poor, sparse, lean, thin, insufficient, inadequate
				v.	1. do without, use frugally/economically 2. let go, not hurt/harm/kill
soothe	*v.*	smooth, ease, placate, quiet, calm, alleviate, relieve, comfort, soften	**sparkle**	*v.*	flash, glitter, glisten, glint, twinkle, gleam, glow, shine, scintillate, shimmer
sore	*a.*	1. painful, hurting, raw, tender, irritated, smarting, aching 2. offended, vexed, cross	**sparse**	*a.*	scanty, meager, spare, poor, lean, thin, insufficient

speak   *v.*   talk, say, tell, state, utter, make an address, orate, discourse, express, voice, declare, proclaim

speed   *n.*   velocity, swiftness, haste, quickness, rapidity, promptness, rate, pace

spell   *n.*   1. charm, incantation
2. attraction, fascination
3. period/space (of time), while, interval

spin   *v.*   revolve, rotate, turn, whirl, twirl, twist

splendid   *a.*   delightful, superb, fine, grand, magnificent, gorgeous, glorious, excellent, brilliant

spoil   *v.*   1. ruin, destroy, damage, harm, hurt, injure, plunder, taint
2. decay, decompose, putrefy, become tainted, rot

         n.   loot, plunder, booty, prizes

sport   *n.*   fun, amusement, pastime, game, pursuit, hobby, pleasure, enjoyment, diversion

spread   *v.*   extend, cover, scatter, distribute, broadcast, transmit, disperse, sow, sprinkle

spring   *v.*   1. flow, run, emerge
2. leap, jump, bound
3. recoil, rebound

spy   *v.*   1. scout, explore, reconnoiter
2. watch, notice, peer

squabble   *v.*   quarrel, bicker

squalid   *a.*   dirty, wretched, miserable, poor, poverty-stricken, disgusting, unpleasant

squeeze   *v.*   press, crush, grip, clasp, embrace, clutch

squirm   *v.*   wriggle, writhe, twist

stab   *v.*   pierce, perforate, puncture, wound

stain   *n.*   1. mark, blemish, blot, smear, disfigurement
2. disgrace, dishonor
3. color, dye, paint

stand   *v.*   1. be upright/erect
2. maintain, support
3. put up with, endure, abide, suffer

         n.   1. stall, booth
2. support, prop, rest
3. firmness, boldness

start   *v.*   1. begin, commence, open, initiate
2. go, set/take off, leave, embark

startle   *v.*   frighten, surprise, shock, alarm, astonish, astound

state   *v.*   say, relate, describe, tell, voice, express, declare

         n.   1. condition, quality
2. country, nation

staunch   *a.*   steadfast, loyal, trustworthy, faithful, devoted, constant, resolute

stay   *v.*   remain, rest, abide, linger, loiter, tarry

         n.   prop, support

steady   *a.*   1. regular, continuous, dependable, reliable, constant, steadfast
2. firm, stable, sturdy, still, calm, composed, certain, sure

steal   *v.*   1. thieve, burgle, rob, loot, plunder, misappropriate, pilfer, purloin, embezzle
2. lurk, sneak, move/travel silently/unnoticed/slyly/furtively

stern   *a.*   strict, harsh, severe, unkind, unbending, inflexible

stiff	*a.*	1. rigid, firm, solid, unbending, immovable, inflexible
		2. not easy, hard, difficult, tough
still	*a.*	calm, motionless, immobile, steady, tranquil, serene, quiet, peaceful, silent
	adv.	however, nevertheless, but
stir	*v.*	move, arouse, rouse, upset, excite, agitate, stimulate
stop	*v.*	1. cease, end, quit, finish, terminate
		2. arrest, halt, check, block
		3. stay, rest, remain, linger, pause
		4. wedge, plug, fill
store	*n.*	1. supply, accumulation, stock
		2. warehouse, shop, magazine, emporium
storm	*n.*	1. wind, gale, tempest
		2. assault, attack, onslaught
		3. bout/fit of anger/fury/rage
story	*n.*	1. tale, yarn, account, anecdote, narrative, description
		2. lie, falsehood, untruth, fib, exaggeration, fabrication
stout	*a.*	1. fat, obese, corpulent, gross, plump
		2. firm, strong, sturdy, tough, lasting, durable, well-built
		3. resolute, staunch, determined, bold, brave, courageous
straight	*a.*	1. level, flat, even, smooth, not bent/curved/crooked
		2. tidy, clear, right, correct
		3. honest, genuine, upright, candid, open, frank, direct, sincere
strange	*a.*	unusual, uncommon, queer, odd, peculiar, eccentric, foreign, alien

strict	*a.*	1. severe, harsh, stern, unbending, inflexible
		2. exact, precise, rigid, accurate
strike	*v.*	1. hit, knock, punch, jab, beat, slap, clout
		2. refuse to work, withhold labor
strive	*v.*	struggle, try, attempt, endeavor
strong	*a.*	1. powerful, vigorous, robust, sturdy, hardy, virile
		2. glaring, brilliant, vivid, dazzling
		3. putrid, rotten, decayed
stubborn	*a.*	obstinate, unbending, unyielding, obdurate, inflexible, headstrong
stumble	*v.*	stagger, blunder, trip, fall, pitch over
stupid	*a.*	foolish, silly, absurd, ridiculous, senseless, dull, unintelligent
sturdy	*a.*	strong, hardy, stalwart, athletic, robust, stout, powerful, vigorous, tough
style	*n.*	fashion, vogue, mode, manner, way, technique, approach
subdue	*v.*	overcome, overpower, quell, crush, conquer, suppress, beat, defeat, master, tame, control
subject	*n.*	1. citizen, dependent
		2. topic, theme
subject	*v.*	expose, make liable to
succeed	*v.*	1. prosper, thrive, flourish
		2. follow, inherit
sudden	*a.*	quick, fast, rapid, swift, speedy, hasty, abrupt, unexpected
suffer	*v.*	1. undergo, bear, stand, put up with, endure, abide
		2. permit, allow, let, tolerate

sufficient   *a.*   enough, ample, adequate, plentiful, abundant, copious

suggestion   *n.*   1. proposal, plan, scheme, proposition, recommendation
2. hint, inkling, clue

suitable   *a.*   appropriate, proper, apt, becoming, befitting, fitting, convenient, satisfactory

superb   *a.*   splendid, marvelous, wonderful, delightful, excellent, magnificent, fine, grand, glorious, gorgeous

supply   *v.*   provide, equip, furnish, give
       n.   store, stock

support   *v.*   1. aid, assist, help, sustain, provide for, befriend, encourage, defend, follow, cooperate with, back, stand by
2. uphold, hold up, prop

suppose   *v.*   fancy, imagine, think, believe, guess, assume, presume

sure   *a.*   1. certain, convinced, confident, positive
2. safe, reliable, dependable

surly   *a.*   sullen, sulky, moody

surprise   *n.*   astonishment, amazement, wonder, shock, bewilderment

surprised   *a.*   startled, shocked, astonished, amazed, astounded, stunned, alarmed, bewildered, flabbergasted, taken aback

surrender   *v.*   give in/up, yield, submit, hand over, capitulate, succumb

surround   *v.*   hem in, encircle, enclose

surroundings   *n.*   environment, locale, neighborhood

suspicious   *a.*   doubtful, dubious, questionable, distrustful, mistrustful

sweet   *a.*   sugary, pleasant, luscious, fragrant, melodious, pleasing, agreeable, fresh, wholesome
       n.   candy, confection, sweetmeat

swell   *v.*   grow bigger/bolder/larger, increase, enlarge, inflate, expand, bulge, bloat

swift   *a.*   quick, fast, rapid, speedy, hasty, hurried, fleet

sympathy   *n.*   understanding, fellow-feeling, compassion

system   *n.*   1. regular method/way, structure, organization, order, plan, scheme, arrangement
2. human body/frame

T t

tab	*n.*	flap, tongue, tag, label, tally
table	*n.*	1. list/summary (of facts/figures), chart 2. flat top, board, slab 3. level area, plain, plateau
tactful	*a.*	prudent, discreet, diplomatic, cautious, careful
taint	*v.*	spoil, blemish, soil, sully, stain, infect, decay, decompose, putrefy, corrupt
take	*v.*	1. remove, abstract, subtract, receive, grasp, seize, arrest, capture 2. lead, conduct, escort
tale	*n.*	story, yarn, account, anecdote, narrative
talent	*n.*	skill, ability, aptitude, gift
talk	*v.*	speak, say, tell, chatter, gossip, discourse, converse, discuss, address, expound, orate
talkative	*a.*	chatty, voluble, garrulous, loquacious
tall	*a.*	high, lofty, elevated, steep, towering
tame	*a.*	timid, docile, subdued, gentle, obedient, not wild, domesticated
tasteful	*a.*	good, pleasing, artistic, stylish, elegant
tasty	*a.*	delicious, savory, piquant, appetizing, sweet, luscious
teach	*v.*	instruct, train, discipline, tutor, coach, educate, inform
tease	*v.*	annoy, irritate, disturb, torment, plague, tantalize, taunt, aggravate
tedious	*a.*	tiresome, wearisome, fatiguing, monotonous, boring, dull
tell	*v.*	say, relate, speak, state, inform, express, voice, disclose, announce, reveal, mention
tempt	*v.*	entice, lure, invite, attract, charm, enchant, captivate, beguile
tender	*a.*	1. soft, gentle, mild, delicate, fragile 2. kind, loving, sympathetic, compassionate 3. sore, painful, aching
	v.	offer, volunteer
terminate	*v.*	end, finish, close, complete, conclude
terrible	*a.*	dreadful, frightful, horrid, frightening, horrible, shocking, awful, terrifying
terrific	*a.*	terrible, awful, frightening, terrifying, huge, immense, enormous, gigantic, tremendous
terrified	*a.*	in terror, very afraid/frightened/scared/alarmed
terror	*n.*	great fear/fright/alarm, dread, horror
test	*v.*	try, examine, check, inspect, investigate
thankful	*a.*	grateful, obliged, indebted
theft	*n.*	robbery, stealing, pilfering, burglary, larceny, piracy
thick	*a.*	1. crowded, swarming, packed, close rank, dense, plentiful, numerous 2. deep, not thin, broad
thin	*a.*	1. not fat, lean, slender, slight, slim, narrow, lanky, gaunt, scrawny, skinny 2. meager, scanty, skimpy, insufficient, inadequate

think	*v.*	1. reason, ponder, consider, meditate, reflect 2. imagine, fancy, believe
thorough	*a.*	complete, entire, full, perfect, exact, accurate
thought	*n.*	belief, idea, notion, view, opinion
thrash	*v.*	beat, belabor, chastise
threaten	*v.*	warn, menace, intimidate, imperil
throw	*v.*	hurl, fling, heave, cast, sling, toss, pitch
tidy	*a.*	neat, clean, orderly, trim
tight	*a.*	stretched, taut, not elastic, secure, firm, steady
tilt	*v.*	slope, slant, incline, lean over
timid	*a.*	tame, shy, reticent, retiring, afraid, apprehensive
tiny	*a.*	very small/little, minute, wee, trifling, trivial, insignificant
tip	*v.*	1. tilt, turn over, upset 2. reward, recompense
tire	*v.*	weary, fatigue, exhaust, bore
tiresome	*a.*	wearisome, boring, tedious, irritating, annoying
toil	*v.*	work, labor, strive, slave
tolerate	*v.*	put up with, allow, let, permit, bear, suffer, abide, overlook, stand for
top	*n.*	highest point/part, summit, head, crown, crest, zenith
torment	*v.*	torture, persecute, tease, badger, plague, distress, annoy, irritate
tough	*a.*	hard, durable, strong, powerful, sturdy, robust, firm, stubborn
tow	*v.*	tug, pull, haul

trace	*v.*	1. seek and find, trail, track, discover 2. mark, copy, reproduce
tradition	*n.*	custom, belief
tragic	*a.*	disastrous, calamitous, sad, sorrowful, unfortunate
train	*v.*	teach, instruct, rear, educate, exercise, bring up, discipline, prepare
tranquil	*a.*	peaceful, calm, composed, untroubled, undisturbed, serene, restful, quiet, still
transform	*v.*	change, alter, convert, turn
transport	*v.*	1. carry, convey, bring 2. delight, enrapture
trap	*n.*	1. snare, ambush, pitfall 2. plot, trick, deception
	v.	catch, capture, snare
travel	*v.*	journey, voyage, move, proceed, progress
treachery	*n.*	disloyalty, betrayal, deceit, trickery
treat	*v.*	1. handle, manage, deal with 2. please, favor, delight
treaty	*n.*	agreement, compact, truce, contract
tremble	*v.*	shake, shiver, shudder, quake, quiver, quaver
tremendous	*a.*	immense, huge, gigantic, enormous, vast, colossal, awe-inspiring
trick	*v.*	1. puzzle, deceive, baffle, mystify, hoax 2. swindle, cheat, defraud
tricky	*a.*	1. artful, crafty, cunning, deceitful, deceptive 2. difficult, risky, dangerous
trip	*n.*	journey, voyage, tour, expedition, outing
triumph	*n.*	success, achievement, victory, win, conquest

rivial	*a.*	trifling, small, little, paltry, petty, slight, insignificant, unimportant
rouble	*n.*	1. bother, worry, vexation, predicament, plight, disaster, distress, calamity
		2. care, effort, pains
	v.	disturb, pester, irritate, molest, distress, upset, annoy, perturb
rue	*a.*	1. real, genuine, actual, authentic
		2. faithful, loyal, reliable, devoted, trustworthy, constant, sincere
rust	*n.*	belief, faith, fidelity, hope, confidence, reliance
rustworthy	*a.*	upright, reliable, faithful, loyal, dependable, honest, truthful

truth	*n.*	honesty, candor, frankness, accuracy
try	*v.*	1. test, check, examine
		2. attempt, endeavor, tackle
tune	*n.*	melody, harmony, song, air
turn	*v.*	1. change, alter, convert
		2. revolve, rotate, roll, spin, whirl, twirl, twist
twist	*v.*	1. wind, turn, rotate, twirl, whirl
		2. curve, bend, change the shape of, contort, distort
tyrant	*n.*	overbearing/cruel master/overseer/overlord, oppressor, despot, dictator

U u

ugly   *a.*   1. not beautiful/handsome/ pretty/lovely, unattractive, unpleasing, repulsive, unsightly, hideous

2. unpleasant, threatening, ill-natured, sinister, dangerous, vile

unable   *a.*   not able, not capable, incapable, powerless

unaware   *a.*   unconscious, without knowledge, unknowing, ignorant, uninformed

uncertain   *a.*   doubtful, dubious, insecure, unsure, undecided, indefinite, unsettled

uncivil   *a.*   impolite, discourteous, rude, bad-mannered, unmannerly

unclean   *a.*   dirty, grimy, tainted, blemished, sullied, soiled, polluted, filthy, foul

uncomfortable   *a.*   disagreeable, uneasy, displeasing, unsure, uneasy

uncommon   *a.*   rare, unusual, remarkable, extraordinary

unconcerned   *a.*   not bothered, unmoved, indifferent, nonchalant

uncouth   *a.*   vulgar, common, rude. boorish, loutish, coarse, ill-mannered, bad-mannered, without courtesy/breeding/ quality/dignity, clumsy, awkward

uncover   *v.*   reveal, disclose, unclothe, disrobe, make bare/naked/ nude

undecided   *a.*   doubtful, dubious, hesitating, hesitant, irresolute, wavering, unsure, uncertain, unsettled

under   *prep.*   beneath, below, inferior to, lower than

undergo   *v.*   experience, put up with, bear, suffer, endure, be subjected to

underhand   *a.*   deceitful, treacherous, sly, crafty, cunning, secret, fraudulent, not straight/ straightforward/aboveboard

understand   *v.*   comprehend, know, grasp, appreciate, perceive, infer

undeserved   *a.*   unmerited, unearned, not deserved

undiscovered   *a.*   hidden, not found, unfound, undisclosed, unrevealed

undisturbed   *a.*   untroubled, cool, calm, confident, sanguine

undoubted   *a.*   not doubtful, certain, sure, undeniable, concrete, absolute

unearth   *v.*   discover, find, uncover, disclose, reveal, recover

uneasy   *a.*   not confident, unsettled, restless, agitated, fidgety, worried, bothered, troubled, concerned, anxious, disturbed, uncomfortable

unequal   *a.*   uneven, unmatched, irregular, unbalanced, different, not alike/the same

unequaled   *a.*   matchless, without peer

uneven   *a.*   rough, coarse, matte, irregular, lopsided, bumpy, undulating

unexpected   *a.*   unforeseen, surprising, unusual

unfair   *a.*   partial, unjust, wrong, wrongful, incorrect, improper, biased

unfaithful   *a.*   disloyal, untrue, deceitful, treacherous, unreliable, untrustworthy

unfasten   *v.*   undo, untie, unbind, unfetter, disconnect, set loose, free, release

unfit	*a.*	1. unsuitable, inappropriate, improper, unqualified, untrained 2. unwell, ill, ailing, sick, bad, unhealthy
unfortunate	*a.*	unlucky, ill-fated, ill-starred, unsuccessful
unfriendly	*a.*	hostile, antagonistic, cold, unreceptive
ungrateful	*a.*	thankless, unthankful, without gratitude
unhappy	*a.*	sad, miserable, sorrowful, gloomy, discontented, dejected, doleful, dismal, distressed, depressed, downcast, despondent
uniform	*a.*	equal, even, the same, similar, alike, constant, regular, consistent, unchanging, fixed, steady, not varied
	n.	dress, costume (of soldier, sailor, policeman, etc.)
unimportant	*a.*	small, slight, trivial, commonplace, mediocre, average, humble, nondescript, insignificant
unit	*n.*	1. one, thing, item, object, article, part, piece, section, group 2. measure
unite	*v.*	join together, combine, amalgamate, bind, marry, fasten/tie together, become one
universal	*a.*	general, widespread, known everywhere, worldwide, international
unjust	*a.*	unfair, incorrect, wrong, wrongful, improper, biased
unkind	*a.*	uncharitable, ungenerous, intolerant, spiteful, vindictive, harsh, cruel
unknown	*a.*	undiscovered, unfound, unexplored, anonymous

unlikely	*a.*	improbable, unsuitable
unlucky	*a.*	unfortunate, ill-fated, unsuccessful
unnecessary	*a.*	unneeded, needless, unwanted, unrequired
unreasonable	*a.*	irrational, illogical, absurd, not sensible
unreliable	*a.*	not dependable, disloyal, unfaithful, untrustworthy
unruly	*a.*	disorderly, undisciplined, disobedient, rowdy, unmanageable
unsatisfactory	*a.*	unsuitable, inappropriate, displeasing, substandard, scratch
unskilled	*a.*	unskillful, inexpert, untalented, untrained, incompetent
untidy	*a.*	disordered, slovenly, scruffy, unkempt, disheveled
until	*prep.*	till, up to, to the time of
untrue	*a.*	1. inaccurate, incorrect, false, counterfeit, erroneous, dishonest 2. unfaithful, disloyal, faithless
unusual	*a.*	not commonplace/ordinary, uncommon, strange, odd, peculiar, eccentric
unwise	*a.*	without wisdom/sagacity/foresight, foolish, rash, reckless, unthinking
unworthy	*a.*	undeserving, dishonorable
upright	*a.*	1. vertical, perpendicular, erect, straight up 2. honest, true, trustworthy, straight
uproar	*n.*	row, commotion, disturbance, chaos
upset	*v.*	1. overturn, topple, knock over, disturb 2. agitate, bother, worry, trouble, be concerned

urge	*v.*	push, press, drive, impel, prod, hasten, beg, beseech, entreat, exhort, pray, implore
urgent	*a.*	pressing, in need of immediate attention, important, serious, grave
use	*v.*	1. employ, utilize, apply, treat 2. consume, exhaust, wear out
useful	*a.*	helpful, advantageous, profitable, gainful, valuable, serviceable
useless	*a.*	ineffectual, unprofitable, ineffective, futile
usual	*a.*	common, ordinary, normal, general, regular, customary
utmost	*a.*	farthest, most distant, greatest, strongest, extreme, uttermost
utter	*v.*	speak, say, voice, declare, assert, blurt, articulate, pronounce, murmur
	a.	complete, total, absolute, sheer, pure, unadulterated, extreme, entire
uttermost	*a.*	farthest, most distant, greatest, strongest, utmost

V v

vacant	*a.*	1. empty, unfilled, deserted, unoccupied, vacated, given up, left open, free 2. dreamy, stupid, foolish, empty-headed, thoughtless, not mentally occupied, not alert/ wide-awake
vacate	*v.*	leave, quit, depart from, give up, abandon, forsake, cease to occupy, go out of, desert
vacation	*n.*	holiday, holiday-time, absence (from work), leave, furlough (soldiers)
vagabond	*n.*	idle wanderer, tramp, rogue, rascal, scoundrel, scamp, harum-scarum, scapegrace, scallywag
vague	*a.*	not clear, indistinct, obscure, ambiguous, uncertain, unsure, indefinite, indeterminate, unsettled, confusing, confused, doubtful, dubious, nebulous, hazy, misty, formless, shapeless, dim
vain	*a.*	1. proud, conceited, bumptious, pompous, egotistical, self-centered, self-satisfied, boastful, self-opinionated, bombastic, vainglorious 2. useless, pointless, futile, purposeless, needless, unnecessary, trivial, insubstantial, empty **in vain:** *without value/ result/reason/purpose*
valiant	*a.*	brave, courageous, fearless, valorous, dauntless, heroic, undaunted, dashing, daring, gallant, bold, unafraid
valley	*n.*	vale, dale, depression, hollow
value	*n.*	1. importance, usefulness, utility, worth, merit, quality, esteem, appreciation, estimation, assessment, appraisal, desirability 2. cost, price, charge, estimate, computation
van	*n.*	1. cart, truck, wagon, coach, carriage 2. advance part, front (of an army or fleet), vanguard
vanish	*v.*	disappear, go/pass out of sight, become invisible, fade away, dissolve, evaporate
vanquish	*v.*	conquer, defeat, beat, be victorious, triumph over, subdue, quell, overcome, overpower, master, quell
variety	*n.*	type, sort, kind, form, class, character, assortment, selection, variation, difference, diversity
various	*a.*	several, a number of, more than one, sundry, miscellaneous, diverse, different, varied, separate
vast	*a.*	very large, great, huge, enormous, gigantic, boundless
vehicle	*n.*	carriage, conveyance/ medium/means for land transport
velocity	*n.*	speed, swiftness, rate, quickness, rapidity, haste, fleetness, pace
vend	*v.*	sell, offer for sale, trade/deal in, retail, peddle
vengeance	*n.*	revenge, retribution, vindictiveness
venture	*n.*	dangerous undertaking, daring/risky exploit/ enterprise/project, adventure

107

verbal	*a.*	oral, vocal, spoken, said, voiced, unwritten	**victim**	*n.*	wrongfully-used person/animal, sufferer, quarry, prey, dupe, gull

verbal *a.* oral, vocal, spoken, said, voiced, unwritten

verdict *n.* decision, judgement, finding, conclusion, opinion, jury's finding/conclusion/judgement/answer

verify *v.* check, examine, test, prove truth/honesty/accuracy/soundness/value/facts of, confirm, bear out

versatile *a.* adaptable, adjustable, changeable, moving freely, capable of/competent in doing many things

vertical *a.* perpendicular, upright, straight up, erect

vessel *n.* 1. container, receptacle, jar, pot, urn, pitcher, beaker, jug, bottle, flask, flagon, phial, vial, pan, can, bin, cask
2. ship, boat

vex *v.* anger, annoy, make irate, provoke, irritate, trouble, afflict, grieve

vibrate *v.* tremble, twitch, shudder, shake, quake, quiver, quaver, rock, agitate, throb, buzz, resound, resonate

vice *n.* wickedness, immorality, wrongdoing, evil, vileness, malignity, malpractice, bad habit, sin, sinfulness, depravity, debauchery, profligacy, license, corruption, fault, defect, blemish

vicious *a.* wicked, immoral, wrongful, evil, vile, malignant, sinful, depraved, distasteful, odious, noxious, corrupt, injurious, spiteful, very unkind, ill-tempered, aggressive, violent, savage, defective, blemished

victim *n.* wrongfully-used person/animal, sufferer, quarry, prey, dupe, gull

victory *n.* conquest, triumph, success, mastery, win, gain, achievement, attainment

view *n.* 1. scene, sight, observation, outlook, setting, vista, panorama
2. opinion, attitude, aim, purpose, intention
v. see, observe, watch, look at/on, regard, survey, scan, inspect, examine
birds-eye view: *overhead view, plan*

viewpoint *n.* standpoint, point of view, opinion, attitude

vigilant *a.* watchful, attentive, wide-awake, alert, aware, cautious, careful, wary, circumspect

vigorous *a.* lively, alive, quick-moving, spry, nimble, energetic, lusty, strenuous, active, animated, brisk, effective, strong, forceful, hard, sharp, powerful, strong, robust, healthy, flourishing, spirited

vile *a.* evil, guilty, wicked, immoral, malignant, sinful, very bad, odious, depraved, corrupt, unpleasant, loathsome, repulsive, distasteful, worthless, base, abject

villain *n.* guilty person, scoundrel, criminal, rogue, rascal, vagabond, wrongdoer, scallywag

violate *v.* 1. attack, despoil, injure, disturb, profane, desecrate, act against, break, treat roughly/badly/unkindly/wrongly/rudely, damage, pollute
2. transgress, infringe

violent	*a.*	forceful, powerful, strong, intense, passionate, vehement, turbulent, raging, angry, furious, fierce, unruly, vindictive, savage, brutal, cruel, aggressive, barbarous, barbaric
virile	*a.*	strong, active, energetic, vigorous, powerful, healthy, full of life, manly, procreative
virtue	*n.*	goodness, excellence, rectitude, righteousness, straightness, purity, morality, good quality, inherent quality/power
visible	*a.*	can be seen/observed/ distinguished/identified, plain, clear, discernible, detectable
vision	*n.*	1. eyesight, perception, discernment 2. imagined sight, image, dream, fantasy, phantom, spirit, ghost, apparition, wraith, specter 3. foresight, insight, ideal, wisdom, sagacity
visit	*v.*	go/come to see, call upon, stay with, frequent
visitation	*n.*	official visit, inspection, long visit, social call, dispensation
vital	*a.*	necessary to/needed for life/existence, very important, essential, much needed
vivacious	*a.*	lively, alive, spirited, sprightly, animated, gay, bright
vivid	*a.*	very clear, glaring, bright, brilliant, intense, strong, forceful, powerful, striking, vigorous, vibrant, unforgettable, true to life

vocal	*a.*	voiced, spoken, said, sung, oral, verbal, vociferous
vogue	*n.*	fashion, mode, popular use/reception/acceptance, present/prevailing/current custom/practice
voice	*v.*	litter, speak, say, express, declare
	n.	say, wish, viewpoint, point of view, opinion
void	*a.*	empty, vacant, useless, ineffectual, lacking, cancelled, null, invalid, not binding
	v.	quit, emit, discharge, evacuate
volume	*n.*	1. capacity, content, size, bulk, mass 2. a roll of parchment, a scroll 3. book, tome
volunteer	*v.*	offer, make a voluntary offer, put forward, undertake, elect, choose
vote	*n.*	ballot, show of hands, election
vouch	*v.*	confirm, bear witness, uphold, guarantee, certify, be surety, underwrite,
vow	*n.*	promise, oath, engagement, undertaking, pledge
voyage	*n.*	sea journey, cruise
vulgar	*a.*	common, prevalent, ill-mannered, bad-mannered, without taste/quality/ manners/breeding, undignified, discourteous, coarse, uncouth, rude, loutish, boorish, plebeian
vulnerable	*a.*	easily wounded/assaulted/ attacked/hurt/assailed, assailable, susceptible to injury, liable to danger, unsafe, unprotected, undefended

Ww

wage	*v.*	carry on, conduct (a war)
wager	*v.*	bet, gamble, back, pledge, promise
wages	*n.*	wage, pay, payment, salary, earnings, income, stipend
wait	*v.*	1. stay, stop, rest, remain, tarry, linger, loiter 2. await, wait/look/watch for, expect, anticipate
waken	*v.*	awaken, awake, wake up, rouse, arouse, stir, bestir
wander	*v.*	stray, roam, ramble, meander, stroll, saunter, amble, digress
wane	*v.*	weaken, diminish, lessen, fail, sink, ebb
want	*v.*	1. desire, wish/crave/long/yearn for 2. lack, need, require
	n.	1. desire, wish, craving, longing, yearning 2. shortage, omission, scarcity, need, poverty, deficiency **in want:** *in need, destitute*
warn	*v.*	give notice, caution, inform/advise/notify of danger, alarm, admonish, threaten
warp	*v.*	1. twist, distort, spoil, disfigure 2. haul, tow (a ship)
wary	*a.*	careful, cautious, wise, prudent, alert, vigilant, watchful
waste	*v.*	1. use/spend unnecessarily/unprofitably/extravagantly, squander, spoil 2. wither, decay, fade
	n.	1. rubbish, refuse, junk, trumpery 2. extravagance, improvidence 3. desert, wilderness
wasteful	*a.*	extravagant, improvident, lavish, thriftless, unthrifty, destructive
watch	*v.*	1. observe, look at, notice, be alert/vigilant/attentive 2. guard, take care of, protect
waver	*v.*	hesitate, be uncertain, demur, vacillate, prevaricate, falter, pause
wax	*v.*	strengthen, increase, expand, enlarge
way	*n.*	1. path, road, route, track, direction 2. method, technique, plan, style, fashion, mode, vogue **by the way:** *by the by, incidentally*
wayward	*a.*	perverse, contrary, awkward, difficult, precocious
weak	*a.*	1. not strong/robust/powerful, feeble, frail, delicate, fragile, sickly, infirm 2. easily influenced, irresolute, shallow
wealth	*n.*	riches, money, fortune, abundance, prosperity, affluence, resources, capital, assets
weary	*a.*	tired, fatigued, exhausted, worn, jaded
	v.	tire, fatigue, exhaust, wear
weep	*v.*	cry, shed tears, sob

weird   *a.*   strange, odd, peculiar, mysterious, uncanny, eerie, unearthly

wet   *a.*   sloppy, sodden, soaked, drenched, moist, damp, humid

whim   *n.*   fancy, idea, notion, craze, caprice

whirl   *v.*   spin, rotate, revolve, turn

white   *a.*   1. pale, pallid, ashen, snowy
2. spotless, clean

whole   *a.*   1. complete, total, full, entire, undivided
2. sound, perfect, healthy

wicked   *a.*   1. evil, sinful, malevolent, malignant, vile, corrupt
2. naughty, mischievous, roguish, bad

wide   *a.*   broad, extensive, vast, spacious

wild   *a.*   1. not tame/domesticated/timid/orderly, untamed, undomesticated, disorderly, savage barbaric, uncivilized
2. waste, uncultivated, uninhabited

wilderness   *n.*   desert, waste, barren/infertile/uncultivated/uninhabited land

willful   *a.*   1. deliberate, intentional
2. obstinate, self-willed, perverse, awkward, stubborn, determined

win   *v.*   get, obtain, gain, earn, acquire, come to possess/own, capture, secure, achieve, procure

wind   *n.*   breeze, gust, blow, gale, air current, draught, breath

wīnd   *v.*   turn, twist, curve, bend, meander, coil, reel

wise   *a.*   sagacious, sensible, clever, intelligent, profound, well-informed, prudent
        n.   way, manner, method, approach

wish   *v.*   want, desire, crave, long, hope, yearn
        n.   desire, craving, longing, yearning, hope

wit   *n.*   1. intelligence, sense, wisdom, understanding, shrewdness, intellect
2. wittiness, humor

withdraw   *v.*   1. go/come away from, retire, retreat, leave, pull/draw out/back, remove
2. recall, take back words/accusation/opinion

withstand   *v.*   resist, oppose

wonder   *v.*   i. marvel, be amazed/surprised/astonished/bewildered
2. doubt, consider, speculate

wonderful   *a.*   marvellous, amazing, astounding, surprising, inspiring, fine, grand, splendid, superb, spectacular, striking, magnificent, awesome

woo   *v.*   court, ask in marriage

work   *n.*   1. labor, effort, toil, task, production
2. job, employment, trade, business, occupation, profession, vocation, calling
3. achievement, feat, deed, product

worn   *a.*   1. used, threadbare, ragged, shabby
2. tired, fatigued, weary, exhausted, jaded

worry	*v.*	bother, trouble, disturb, irritate, tease, tantalize, torment, annoy, sadden	
	n.	problem, care, anxiety, burden	
worship	*v.*	revere, respect, idolize, venerate, praise, laud, glorify, adore, deify	
worth	*n.*	value, cost, price, merit, excellence, importance, benefit	
worthless	*a.*	of no worth/value/merit, without worth/value/merit/ excellence, valueless, useless, pointless	
worthy	*a.*	honest, true, upright, decent, righteous, good, worthwhile, admirable, excellent	
wound	*v.*	hurt, injure, maim, upset, grieve	
wrath	*n.*	anger, rage, fury, ire, vexation, annoyance, indignation	
wreck	*v.*	1. ruin, destroy, disable, blight, spoil	
		2. be shipwrecked	
	n.	1. ruined/emaciated/ dissipated/unhealthy person	
		2. shipwreck, wrecked ship	

wreckage *n.* remains, debris, remnants, fragments, flotsam

wretched *a.* 1. sad, dejected, miserable, unhappy, afflicted, woeful, discontented, pathetic, pitiful, pitiable
2. mean, contemptible, unworthy, despised, shabby, poor, impoverished

writhe *v.* 1. twist, wriggle, squirm, reel, roll
2. be stung/annoyed

wrong *a.* 1. wrongful, not right, incorrect, inaccurate, improper, unsuitable
2. bad, wicked, immoral, evil, vicious, sinful, unjust, unfair, illegal, unlawful
n. injury, misdeed, sin, evil, vice, wickedness, injustice
v. injure, damage, hurt, harm, abuse, treat unfairly/unjustly

wry *a.* twisted, crooked, distorted, askew
awry: *crookedly, distortedly*

112

X-rays   *n.*   penetrating rays, Roentgen
                          rays
                          X-ray: *X-ray examination/*
                          photograph

Xmas   *n.*   (abbreviation for) Christmas,
                        the Christmas season,
                        Christmas-tide,
                        Christmas-time, the
                        Christmas feast/festival,
                        yule, yule-tide

Y y

yank	*v.*	jerk, pull sharply/quickly/suddenly/forcibly/forcefully, snatch
yarn	*n.*	story, tale, anecdote, account, narrative
yearn	*v.*	long, crave, desire greatly/strongly, want very much, wish, hanker, pine
yell	*v.*	bawl, cry out/loudly/shrilly, shout loudly/suddenly, scream, blare, blast
yelp	*n.*	loud yap, shrill bark, sharp/loud cry
yet	*adv.*	1. still, until/up to then/now, this/the present time, at present, at that/this time, so far, in the near future 2. also, in addition, again, further 3. however, nevertheless, despite that/this, in spite of that/this, but for all that, but at the same time

yield	*v.*	1. give up/in, surrender, submit, relinquish, resign, hand/deliver over 2. give, produce, supply, provide, deliver
	n.	product, supply, output, amount/quantity produced, crop, harvest
young	*a.*	youthful, juvenile, not adult/grown-up, immature
youngster	*n.*	child, juvenile, young person, minor
youth	*n.*	young man, teenage boy/lad, male adolescent
yule	*n.*	yuletide, Christmas (Xmas), Christmas-tide, Christmas-time, the Christmas feast/festival/season

Z z

zeal   *n.*   enthusiasm, eagerness, ardor, passion, devotion, determination, keenness, fervor, fanaticism, earnestness, zest, verve, vigor, intensity

zealot   *n.*   zealous person, fanatic, extremist

zero   *n.*   1. nothing, nought, nil
2. startingpoint (on a scale)
3. figure *0*, cipher
zero-hour: *1. twelve o'clock (midnight)*
2. fixed/pre-arranged starting-time

zest   *n.*   great enjoyment, keen interest, relish, gusto, enthusiasm, eagerness, passion, keenness, fervor, zeal, vigor, vim, verve, vivacity

zigzag   *a.*   with alternate right and left turns/angles, with a series of sharp bends, jagged, barbed, twisted, crooked, winding

zip   *n.*   1. energy, vigor, verve, rapid action, fast movement, great motion, high speed, zest, vim, vivacity
2. light/sharp/bullet-like/ tearing sound
3. zip-fastener

zone   *n.*   belt, girdle, space, region
It is extremely cold in Earth's frigid **zones**.

zoom   *v.*   move/climb noisily and speedily
The airplane **zoomed** into the clouds.

115

Supplement
Opposites

abandon 1. keep, retain, hold, remain in, occupy, take over 2. restraint, caution, care
abandoned 1. kept, retained, occupied, owned 2. restrained, restricted, cautious
abate increase, strengthen, begin, start
abduct 1. return 2. care for, protect, guard
abhor like, love, admire, cherish
abide 1. go/depart from 2. reject, dismiss
ability inability, incompetence, inefficiency
able unable, incompetent, ineffective, weak
abnormal normal, usual, regular, ordinary
abolish establish, validate, allow, permit
above below, beneath, lower than, under
aboveboard dishonest, deceitful, suspicious
abroad near, here, not distant, at home
abrupt gradual, slow, gentle, courteous
absent present, here, in existence
absolute imperfect, incomplete, restricted
absorb exude, emit, give off/out
abstain participate, indulge/join in
abstract real, concrete, feasible, practical
absurd sound, sensible, logical, reasonable
abundance scarcity, shortage, paucity
abuse care for, treat properly, respect
accelerate decelerate, slow down, retard, impede
accept reject, refuse, decline, dismiss
access way out, exit, outlet
accommodate not help/serve, hinder, withhold
accompany disregard, ignore, avoid
accomplice enemy, opponent, adversary
accomplish fail, give up/in, relinquish
accumulate disperse, scatter, lose, spend
accurate inaccurate, inexact, doubtful
achieve fail, lose, give up, forsake
acknowledge 1. ignore 2. deny, refuse, reject
acquaint conceal, keep confidential
acquire lose, give away, reject, refuse
action inactivity, inaction, laziness
active inactive, slow, idle, slothful
actual unreal, abstract, false, fictitious

acute obtuse, low, soft, mild, dull
adamant yielding, resilient, flexible
add subtract, deduct, decrease, remove
adequate inadequate, insufficient, not enough
adhere be separated/loosened/detached
adjacent far, distant, detached, apart, separate
adjust disarrange, disorder
admire disapprove, dislike, condemn
admit deny, disallow, repudiate
adopt disown, forsake, abandon, desert
adore dislike, detest, hate, abhor, loathe
adrift fixed, moored, tied-up, fastened
adult 1. child, youngster 2. immature, childish
advance 1. withdraw, retreat 2. decline, worsen
advantage disadvantage, hindrance, handicap
adversary friend, ally, accomplice, assistant
advertise conceal, hide, camouflage, cover up, disguise
affection dislike, hatred, aversion, abhorrence
afford 1. unable to buy 2. withhold
afloat sunk, on shore, not at sea
afraid brave, courageous, bold, fearless
age 1. youth 2. rejuvenate
agile awkward, slow, sluggish, clumsy
agitate calm, quiet, soothe, relieve
agony joy, gladness, pleasure, delight
agree disagree, refuse, oppose, disapprove
agreeable disagreeable, unpleasant, nasty
agreement disagreement, opposition
ahead behind, retarded, late, tardy
aid 1. hindrance, opposition 2. hinder, impede
alarm 1. calm, peace 2. soothe, quiet, pacify, console
alert 1. inattentive, dreamy, absentminded 2. sluggish, slow, inactive, lethargic
alight fly off, ascend, mount, get on
alike not alike/the same, dissimilar, different
allow disallow, forbid, ban, refuse, deny
alone accompanied/in company
alter preserve, keep, maintain, retain
amateur expert, master, specialist, professional
ambition aimlessness, indifference, disinterest
amend spoil, destroy, injure, impair
amiable unfriendly, ill-tempered, moody
ample inadequate, insufficient, short, deficient
amuse displease, bore, weary

anger please, delight, charm, amuse

announce conceal, hide, withhold, cover up

annoy please, amuse, charm, soothe

answer 1. question, query 2. ask, request

anticipate neglect, forget, disregard

anxiety peace, calm, contentment

apart together, adjacent, close, near

apparent 1. real, actual 2. doubtful, unlikely

appeal deny, refuse, repudiate

appear disappear, vanish

applaud condemn, disapprove, decry

appreciation 1. disapproval, misunderstanding 2. depreciation, fall in value

approach departure, way out, exit

appropriate inappropriate, unsuitable

approve disapprove, condemn, decry

apt 1. inappropriate, unsuitable 2. badly put/chosen, unimpressive

argue agree, concur, consent

arouse calm, quiet, soothe, mollify

arrange disarrange, disorder, scatter

arrest release, let go, free

ascend descend, fall, come/go down

ashamed unashamed, unabashed

ask reply, retort, answer, tell

assault retreat, withdrawal

assemble dismiss, disperse, scatter

assist hinder, impede, delay

associate 1. disassociate, compete 2. competitor, rival

assume relinquish, give up, avoid

astray 1. on course, direct 2. found

attach detach, unfasten, sever, disconnect

attachment dislike, aversion, animosity

attack retreat, withdraw, fall back

attain fail, lose, fall short of

attempt avoid, evade, shirk, disregard

attend ignore, disregard, be absent from

attire disrobe, undress, unclothe

attract repel, repulse, displease

audacity timidity, shyness, reticence

authentic unreliable, sham, false

avail hinder, impede, delay

available out of reach, distant, inconvenient

avarice generosity, unselfishness, benevolence

average unusual, exceptional, out of the ordinary, uncommon, extraordinary

aversion love, fondness, affection

avert accept, receive, tolerate

avoid accept, receive, meet, confront, frequent

awake 1. fall asleep 2. asleep, sleeping

aware unconscious, unaware, unknowing

away near, close, here, ·present, at home

awe irreverence, disrespect, indifference

awkward 1. graceful, elegant 2. easy, simple

babyish adult, mature, grown-up

back 1. front, fore part, front side 2. advance, progress 3. hinder, impede

backward 1. beforehand, forward, in advance 2. bright, smart, intelligent

bad 1. good, obedient, moral, virtuous 2. rich, superior, pleasing, pure 3. well, healthy

baffle enlighten, instruct, inform

balance 1. imbalance 2. make unequal

ban allow, permit, tolerate, institute

band single, lone, individual

banish call/bring back, recall

bar allow, permit, tolerate, accept

bare covered, clothed, adorned, ample

barely amply, sufficiently, quite

barren fruitful, fertile, full, profitable

base 1. top, summit 2. admirable, noble

bashful forward, bold, brazen

battle peace, agreement, truce

bear 1. collapse under 2. disallow

beautiful ugly, unattractive, repulsive

become 1. remain, cease to be 2. ill adorn

becoming unsuitable, inappropriate, unbecoming

before after, behind, late

befriend alienate, be hostile to, hinder

beg give, allow, grant, consider

beggarly 1. abundant, adequate 2. rich, wealthy

begin cease, finish, end, terminate

behind before, beforehand, in advance, ahead, in good time

belief disbelief, doubt, uncertainty

belong not belong, be separate/apart, inapplicable

below above, on top, superior to, higher than

bend straighten, level, unbend

beneath above, higher than, superior to

benefit disadvantage, burden, loss

benevolent unhelpful, miserly, ill-disposed

beside distant/far/apart from, detached, separate

best worst, most unsuitable/debased

better worse, less preferable/desirable

bewilder enlighten, instruct, inform

beyond near, close, here, inside

bicker agree, concur, consent

big small, little, trivial, unimportant

bind unbind, unfasten, untie, set free

bitter sweet, luscious, pleasing, pleasant

blame praise, commend, applaud

blank full, occupied, written/printed on

blatant quiet, peaceful, disguised, concealed

bleak bright, brilliant, interesting, attractive

blend disunite, separate, disharmonize

blessed cursed, defiled, unfortunate, ill-favored

blind 1. seeing 2. knowing, aware, appreciative

block open, empty, support, help

bloodthirsty peaceful, tame, civilized

blunder diplomatic/sensible/correct/wise act/ action

blurred distinct, clear, unstained

boast humility, reticence

bogus genuine, real, true, authentic

bold timid, shy, nervous, afraid

bondage freedom, liberty

bore interest, amuse, entertain, beguile

borrow lend, provide a loan, give, impart

boundless bounded, limited, restricted, finite

bravado timidity, humility, modesty

brave afraid, frightened, cowardly

brawny skinny, weak, frail

break 1. join, unite 2. mend, repair

brief long, lengthy, comprehensive

bright 1. dull, dim, faded 2. backward, slow

brilliant 1. dull, drab 2. retarded, stupid

bring leave, take, remove, return

brisk slow, lazy, idle, retarded

brittle strong, secure, tough, durable

broad narrow, slender, slim, closed

broadcast gather, collect, assemble

brutal kind, considerate, merciful

build dismantle, demolish, destroy

bully encourage, soothe, protect

bumptious humble, meek, modest, unpretentious

burn extinguish, put out

busy inactive, unoccupied, unemployed, dilatory, idle

buy sell, vend, peddle

call listen, hear, attend

calm disturbed, agitated, upset, uneasy

camouflage reveal, expose, uncover, display

cancel allow, keep, approve, support

capable incapable, incompetent, inefficient

capture free, release, liberate, rescue

care 1. neglect, carelessness, unconcern 2. unwariness, imprudence

careless careful, cautious, thoughtful, mindful

carry release, put down, drop

cast 1. catch, grab, pick up 2. deform, misshape

casual careful, cautious, formal, orderly

catch 1. cast, throw 2. miss 3. release, rescue

cause 1. effect, result 2. prevent

cautious incautious, careless, unwary, imprudent

cease begin, commence, start, initiate

ceaseless ceasing, ending, interrupted

celebrate disregard, ignore, overlook, forget

center outside, exterior, external part

certain uncertain, unsure, indefinite

challenge agreement, acceptance, compliance

champion 1. loser 2. rival 3. poorest, worst

chance certainty, design

change remain, keep, maintain

chaos order, system, method

charge 1. withdrawal, retreat 2. praise, commend, excuse, pardon charm repel, displease, disenchant

cheap costly, dear, high-priced, valuable

cheat protect, cover, be honest with

check 1. speed up, accelerate 2. ignore, disregard

cheek respect, regard, consideration

cheer 1. displease, dishearten, discourage 2. jeer, decry, condemn

chief 1. unimportant, insignificant 2. follower, subordinate

child adult, grown-up, mature person

chill 1. hot, warm 2. friendly, emotional

choose ignore, disregard, disown

claim reject, disregard, disown
clamp unclasp, release, free
clean dirty, soiled, impure, untidy
clear indistinct, dull, dim, vague
clever ignorant, stupid, foolish, untalented
climb descend, go/come down
cloak reveal, disclose, unmask
close open, unfold, begin
clown 1. act/behave sensibly/wisely 2. sage
clumsy agile, graceful, careful, skillful
clutch release, let go, free, liberate
coarse 1. smooth, polished 2. polite, civil
coax discourage, dissuade, dishearten
coil uncoil, unwind, unwrap
cold 1. warm, hot 2. close, affectionate
collapse build, erect, construct
collect disperse, broadcast, scatter
collide separate, go apart, part
colossal small, tiny, miniature
combat peace, lull, truce
combine separate, split, divide
come leave, go, quit, depart
comfort 1. discomfort 2. discourage, dishearten
comic tragic, serious, dignified
command obey, follow, accept
commence finish, end, stop, conclude
commit 1. cease, fail 2. recall, receive
common uncommon, unusual, extraordinary
companion enemy, opponent, antagonist
company 1. individual 2. privacy
compare contrast, differ
compel prevent, preclude
compete help, assist, cooperate
competent incompetent, incapable, unskilled
complain praise, commend, approve
complete 1. initiate, begin 2. incomplete, partial
compliment criticize, blame, insult
compose 1. break up, scatter 2. disturb
conceal disclose, uncover, reveal, expose
conceit humility, humbleness, meekness, simplicity
concentrate 1. daydream 2. scatter, spread
concern calm, composure, unconcern
conclude begin, start, open, initiate
condemn praise, approve, commend, pardon

condense expand, lengthen, extend
conduct misconduct, mislead, misdirect
confess conceal, hide, cover up
confident uncertain, unsure, insecure
confidential open, revealed, disclosed
confine release, free, discharge
confuse 1. arrange, order 2. enlighten, inform
connect disconnect, unfasten, untie
conquer lose, fail, surrender, give in
consider disregard, ignore, scorn
considerable small, meager, insufficient
considerate unkind, selfish, spiteful
construct dismantle, pull down, destroy
consume 1. yield, create 2. collect, gather
content discontent, unhappiness, displeasure
contest peace, harmony, cooperation
continue discontinue, cease, conclude
contract expand, enlarge, extend, inflate
contradict agree with, allow, grant
control mismanage, misdirect, mislead
convenient inconvenient, unsuitable, inappropriate
cool 1. warm, hot 2. rash, emotional
core outside, outer part
correct incorrect, wrong, inaccurate
correspond disagree, differ, vary
costly cheap, inexpensive, low-priced
couple disunite, disconnect, uncouple
courage cowardice, fear, timidity
courtesy discourtesy, rudeness, impoliteness
cover uncover, reveal, disclose, expose
crafty honest, straightforward, frank, sincere
cram empty, discharge, remove, release
crazy sensible, reasonable, logical, sane
credit discredit, dishonor, disgrace
criminal innocent, virtuous, legal, lawful
crisp soft, tender, flabby
criticize praise, applaud, commend
cross 1. support, agree with 2. please, charm
crowd 1. individual, single, solitary 2. disperse
crude 1. refined, polished 2. genteel, courteous
cruel kind, gentle, considerate, compassionate
crust inside, interior, core, center, kernel, heart
cry laugh, grin, chuckle

cultivate 1. reap, gather, harvest 2. destroy, reject, lay waste

cunning honest, frank, open, sincere

curious 1. indifferent, uninterested 2. ordinary, normal

current out-of-date, old-fashioned, obsolete

curse bless, sanctify, praise, commend

customer seller, vendor, shopkeeper

daily rarely, infrequently, irregularly

dainty indelicate, inelegant, coarse

damage repair, mend, fix, preserve, protect

damp 1. dry, arid 2. encourage

danger safety, security

dare play safe, accept, comply

daring shy, timid, afraid, cowardly

dark bright, light, vivid, clear, sunny, cheerful

dart dawdle, linger, loiter

dash 1. loiter, linger, dawdle

dawn 1. nightfall, sunset 2. end, finish

day night, night-time

dead alive, living, alert, sensitive

deaden increase awareness/vitality, amplify

deadly healthy, life-giving, stimulating

deaf 1. able to hear 2. attentive, mindful

deal collect, gather, hoard, store

dear cheap, inexpensive, low-priced

debate agree, concur, cooperate

debt credit, gain, benefit

deceive be honest/truthful/straight, undeceive

decent indecent, improper, vulgar, unseemly

decide delay, postpone, unsettle

declare conceal, hide, cover up, disguise

decline 1. accept 2. increase, rise, improve

decorate deface, disfigure, mar, spoil

decrease increase, enlarge, expand

defeat 1. surrender, submit 2. victory, conquest

defect improvement, advantage

defend 1. desert, leave, abandon 2. attack, assault

definite uncertain, indistinct, indefinite

deformed shapely, graceful, elegant

defraud reward, pay, recompense

delay advance, accelerate, hasten, hurry

deliberate unintentional, impetuous, hasty

delicate 1. strong, tough 2. uncouth, coarse

delicious bitter, nasty, unpalatable, unsavory

delight displease, sadden, disappoint

deliver keep back, retain, return

demand give, hand over, offer, present

demolish construct, erect, build, restore

dense 1. thin, scanty, sparse 2. intelligent

deny admit, allow, accept, grant

depart remain, wait, stay, return

depression 1. mound, hillock 2. happiness

derelict occupied, well-kept

descend go/get up, rise, mount, ascend

descent rise, ascent, climb

desert 1. occupy, inhabit 2. fertile, fruitful

deserve be unworthy/undeserving of

desirable undesirable, unwanted, unattractive

desire reject, dislike, disregard

despair hope, encouragement, optimism

desperate 1. calm, composed 2. hopeful, confident

despise like, love, approve of, commend

destroy make, build, create, renew

detach attach, fasten, tie, join, unite

detain release, set free, liberate, deliver

detect not notice, pass over/by, miss

determined irresolute, undecided, undetermined

detest like, love, cherish, care for

develop contract, condense, shorten, reduce

devoted disloyal, unfaithful, inconstant, indifferent

dictate follow orders, ask, beg, beseech, pray

die live, survive, flourish

different similar, alike, the same

difficulty help, assistance, ease, comfort

dignity humility, simplicity, informality

diligent lazy, idle, careless, slothful

dim bright, clear, conspicuous

din quiet, silence, calm, tranquillity

dingy clean, bright, unfaded

dip mound, hill, rise, upwards slope

direct indirect, round-about, circuitous

dirt cleanliness, tidiness

disaster blessing, benefit, boon

discipline indiscipline, disorder, unruliness

disgrace honor, favor, praise

disguise reveal, uncover, unmask, unveil

isgusting agreeable, pleasing, charming
ismal bright, cheerful, gay, pleasant
ismiss employ, engage, admit, assemble
isplace arrange, order, adjust, group
isplay hide, cover, conceal, camouflage
isplease please, charm, beguile, amuse
istant 1. near, close 2. friendly, sociable
istinct 1. indistinct, vague 2. connected
istress pleasure, gladness, comfort
istribute collect, gather, keep, store
istrust trust, confidence, faith, belief
isturb calm, quiet, soothe, appease
ivide join, unite, combine, mix, bind
lodge meet, approach, confront
lonate receive, take, retain, accept
loubtful certain, sure, definite, decided
lrab bright, exciting, vivid, cheerful
lrag push, shove, thrust
lrain fill, replenish
lrastic mild, moderate, feeble
lraw push, shove, thrust
lreadful pleasing, pleasant, harmless, innocuous
lreary bright, cheerful, exciting, pleasing
lress undress, disrobe
lrive discourage, dissuade, restrain
lrop lift, raise, ascend, elevate
lrown increase, amplify, intensify
lrowsy wide-awake, alert
lry wet, damp, moist, soaked, humid
lual 1. single 2. manifold
lue undeserved, unsuitable, inappropriate
lull 1. interesting 2. bright 3. intelligent
    4. keen
luty pleasure, leisure, irresponsibility
lwell leave, quit, vacate, abandon
lwindle increase, enlarge, multiply
lye leave natural color, bleach
each all
eager indifferent, uninterested, shy
early 1. recent, present 2. late, behind
earn lose, forfeit, give up
ease 1. discomfort, trouble 2. aggravate, increase
easy difficult, hard, involved
eccentric normal, ordinary, sensible
edge center, middle

effect 1. cause, origin 2. neglect, overlook
effective 1. incapable, incompetent
    2. unimpressive
efficient incompetent, ineffective
effort ease, rest, relaxation
elaborate 1. plain, simple 2. simplify
elapse stand/remain still
elastic inelastic, inflexible, rigid, stiff
elated sad, gloomy, miserable
elect dismiss, reject. disregard, ignore
elegant awkward, ungainly, inelegant
elementary advanced, difficult, complex
eliminate keep, retain, maintain, preserve
eloquent uncommunicative, unimpressive,
    inarticulate
embark disembark, return
embarrass assure, comfort
embrace 1. unclasp 2. exclude
emerge submerge, retreat, hide
emergency 1. routine, regular, normal 2. security
eminent unknown, obscure, nondescript
employ dismiss, sack, discharge, fire
empty 1. fill, replenish 2. full, occupied
enchant disenchant, displease, offend
encounter avoid, evade, dodge
encourage discourage, dishearten
end begin, start, commence, open, cause
endanger make safe/secure
endless brief, short, limited
endure give in, yield, surrender
enemy friend, ally, companion
energetic inactive, lethargic, lazy
engage 1. dismiss, discharge 2. withdraw
enjoyment sadness, misery, unhappiness
enlarge diminish, decrease, reduce
enlighten 1. darken 2. baffle, confuse
enormous little, small, tiny, miniature
enough insufficient, inadequate, poor
enrage placate, pacify, please, charm
enter go out, quit, depart from, vacate
entertain bore, weary, irritate
enthusiasm unconcern, indifference
entice repel, reject, disregard, ignore
entire partial, incomplete, fragmentary
entrance exit, way out, retreat

envy tolerance, acceptance, goodwill
equal unequal, different, differing
equivalent not alike, dissimilar, unequal
erase keep, retain, restore
erect 1. lower, take apart 2. horizontal, flat
error correction, amendment
escape 1. remain, stay 2. meet, confront
escort disregard, mislead, misguide
essential inessential, dispensable, unimportant
establish disestablish, dissolve, destroy
eternal brief, short, limited
evade meet, encounter, confront
evaporate materialize, appear
even uneven, odd, inexact, irregular
eventually firstly, immediately, directly
everlasting brief, short, limited
evident obscure, indistinct, concealed
evil virtue, goodness, justice
exact inexact, inaccurate, incorrect
exaggerate understate, be realistic
examine ignore, disregard, avoid
exasperate please, soothe, satisfy
exceed fall/go below/behind
excel fail, lose, falter, be inferior
excellent poor, inferior, bad
exceptional unexceptional, ordinary
excess shortage, lack, deficiency
excite calm, quiet, soothe, pacify
exclude include, leave/keep in
excuse accuse, blame, condemn
exertion inactivity, rest, relaxation
exhaust 1. refresh, invigorate 2. replenish
exhibit conceal, cover, hide
exist die out, pass away, fade, wither, perish
exit entrance, way in, inlet
expend decrease, contract, deflate
expel admit, enter, absorb, take in
expense profit, gain, income
expensive cheap, inexpensive, low-priced
experience inexperience, ignorance
expert 1. inexpert, unskilled 2. amateur, beginner, novice
expose conceal, hide, cover
express suppress, withhold, conceal
exquisite unattractive, ugly, displeasing

extend 1. shorten, contract 2. receive, take
exterior interior, inside, internal, inner
exterminate protect, preserve, conserve
external interior, inside, internal, inner
extract return, push/pull/put back
extraordinary ordinary, common, usual, unimportant
extravagance thrift, economy, care
fabulous 1. factual, authentic 2. simple, ordinary, commonplace
fade grow, flourish, revive, increase
fail 1. pass, succeed 2. improve, flourish
faint 1. clear, distinct 2. strong, vigorous
fair 1. unfair, unjust 2. ugly, unattractive 3. dull, inclement 4. unsatisfactory, not acceptable
faithful disloyal, inconstant, unreliable
fake real, true, genuine, authentic, original
fall 1. rise, ascend 2. increase, appreciate
false 1. real, genuine 2. correct, right 3. loyal, faithful, trustworthy
familiar 1. unknown, uncommon, rare 2. formal, distant, unfriendly
famous unknown, obscure, unimportant, nondescript
fancy 1. fact, reality, truth 2. plain, simple, not decorative
far near, close, adjacent, handy
farther nearer, closer
fascinate repel, displease, disenchant
fast 1. slow, sluggish, lethargic 2. loose, insecure 3. feed, feast, eat
fasten detach, untie, disconnect, uncouple
fat thin, lean, slim, skinny
fatal harmless, safe, innocuous
fatigue revive, strengthen, enliven, exhilarate, invigorate 2. freshness, vigor
favorable unfriendly, unhelpful, unkind, not well-disposed, unfavorable
fear courage, bravery, boldness, confidence
feeble strong, powerful, robust, firm
feminine masculine, male, manly
ferocious meek, timid, gentle, tame, docile
fetch return, take/send back
fierce meek, timid, gentle, tame, mild
fill empty, drain, deplete, exhaust, vacate
final first, opening, initial, primary

ind lose, mislay, waste

ine 1. coarse, crude, poor 2. dull, wet, inclement 3. reward, payment, bonus

inish begin, commence, start, open, initiate

it unfit, unsuitable, inappropriate

ix 1. detach, disconnect 2. damage, ruin 3. unsettle, cancel

lat 1. uneven, perpendicular, hilly 2. lively, vivacious

lee return, come/go back, remain, stay

lexible inflexible, rigid, unbending, implacable

ling catch, grab, clutch, clasp, hold

loat sink, settle, descend, alight

lourish do badly, wither, fade, wane, decline

'oe friend, ally, companion, comrade

'oggy clear, plain, distinct

'ollow 1. lead, guide, direct 2. ignore, disregard 3. misunderstand, not comprehend 4. precede, go before

'ool 1. sage, genius, expert 2. be serious/honest

'oolhardy prudent, thoughtful, cautious, careful

forbid allow, permit, tolerate

force 1. discourage, restrain 2. weakness, delicacy, gentleness

foreign familiar, known, native

forget remember, recall, recollect

forgive blame, accuse, charge, condemn

forlorn happy, contented, satisfied

former latter, following, succeeding

forsake keep, retain, maintain, own

fortunate unfortunate, unlucky, ill-fated

fortune 1. certainty 2. poverty

foul 1. fair, tasteful, pleasant 2. clean, pure

fraction whole, full amount, total

fragile strong, sturdy, robust, firm

frantic calm, composed, undisturbed, nonchalant

free 1. capture, seize, imprison, arrest 2. ungenerous, illiberal 3. restrained

frequent rare, uncommon, infrequent, few

friendly unfriendly, hostile, antagonistic

frighten calm, soothe, comfort, pacify

front back, rear, posterior

fruitful infertile, barren, unprofitable

full 1. empty, vacant 2. incomplete, partial

funny serious, grave, sober, dignified

furious calm, composed, gentle, placid

futile effective, profitable, worthwhile

gain 1. lose, mislay 2. decrease, reduce

gallant timid, afraid, frightened, cowardly

game 1. work, employment 2. hunter, predator 3. timid, cowardly 4. agile, uninjured

gather scatter, distribute, disperse

gaudy dull, dark, drab, dreary

gaunt plump, fat, fleshy, flabby

gay serious, gloomy, mournful, depressed

gaze glance, glimpse

general unusual, uncommon, rare, irregular

generous 1. illiberal, mean, miserly 2. insufficient, inadequate

genial ungenial, unsociable

gentle 1. harsh, rough, unkind, brutal 2. dishonorable, not genteel, vulgar

genuine false, sham, fake, counterfeit, unsound, insincere, dishonest

get lose, return, reject, give back

ghastly pleasing, charming, attractive

giant small, tiny, miniature, minute, dwarf

giddy 1. steady, stable, sober 2. constant, reliable

gigantic small, tiny, miniature, minute

give receive, take, accept, return

glad 1. sad, displeased, unhappy 2. dull, ugly, dreary, cheerless

glamorous ugly, unattractive, plain, simple

glance gaze, watch, stare

glare 1. dullness, dimness 2. smile, grin

glimpse gaze, watch, stare

gloomy happy, joyful, gay, cheerful

glorious shameful, unworthy, dishonorable

glossy dull, dim, unpolished, lusterless

glum happy, joyful, gay, cheerful

glutton abstemious eater/person

go 1. come, return 2. stand/remain still 3. be out of action/inactive/motionless

good 1. untrue, improper, unjust, immoral, bad, corrupt, unsatisfactory, inadequate, poor, ungenerous 2. unfavorable, unprofitable, unhelpful, inefficient, adulterated, tainted, inferior 3. unskilled, untalented, stupid

gorgeous simple, plain, dull, drab, dreary

govern 1. misgovern, mismanage 2. obey, follow

grab return, give back, fling, throw

graceful ungraceful, inelegant, unattractive

gracious discourteous, unmannerly, disagreeable

gradual fast, quick, rapid, sudden, abrupt
grand poor, inferior, ordinary, commonplace
grant 1. take, receive 2. disallow, prohibit, refuse
grasp 1. release, let go 2. misunderstand, not comprehend
grateful ungrateful, unthankful, unacceptable
great small, little, poor, inferior, ordinary, commonplace, unimportant, insignificant, unknown, undistinguished
greedy generous, liberal, openhanded
greet ignore, disregard, not acknowledge
grief 1. happiness, joy, contentment 2. good fortune
grip release, unclasp, let go, free
groan laugh, praise, applaud, commend
gross 1. small, little, lean, thin 2. refined, clean, delicate 3. indistinct, concealed, hidden 4. net, after deductions
ground 1. sky, heavens 2. top, roof
grow wither, fade, decrease, shrink, contract
grown-up childish, puerile, youthful, immature
gruesome pleasant, pleasing, attractive, elegant
grumble commend, praise, applaud
guess know, be certain/sure/confident
guide 1. misguide, mislead, misdirect 2. follow, obey
guile honesty, truthfulness, frankness, candor
gullible shrewd, astute, discerning
habitual rare, seldom, irregular, infrequent
haggard fresh, lively, energetic, untroubled
hail ignore, disregard, avoid
halt start, begin, commence, go, advance, proceed
hamper encourage, aid, help, assist, support
handicap advantage, help, aid, assistance, benefit
handsome ugly, unattractive, ungraceful
handy useless, inconvenient, awkward, clumsy, remote
haphazard orderly, settled, planned, organized
happy sad, miserable, dejected, unhappy
harass aid, help, support, soothe, please
hard 1. soft, yielding 2. sympathetic, kind 3. easy, not difficult
hardship good fortune, pleasure, benefit
hardy weak, feeble, frail, fragile, delicate

harm help, assist, benefit, please, improve
harmless harmful, hurtful, damaging, injurious
harsh 1. easy, kind, sensitive 2. soft, pleasant, agreeable
harvest sow, set, broadcast, scatter
hasty 1. slow, unhurried 2. careful, considerate
hate like, love, admire, adore, cherish
hateful pleasing, pleasant, likeable, lovable, amiable
haughty humble, unassuming, simple, shy
haul push, shove, thrust, drive
have 1. disown 2. give up, relinquish, repudiate, reject, forfeit 3. refuse to allow/permit
hazard 1. safety, safeguard 2. certainty, guarantee
hazy clear, plain, distinct, bright
headlong 1. feet first/foremost 2. carefully, thoughtfully
headstrong careful, cautious, prudent, irresolute
heal damage, injure, harm, hurt
healthy unhealthy, ailing, infirm, sickly, unsound, unwholesome
heap scatter, spread, disperse, broadcast
heart exterior, outside, crust
heartless feeling, gentle, kind, sympathetic
hearty 1. unfriendly, unsociable 2. insincere, hypocritical 3. weak, delicate
heat 1. cold, coldness, coolness 2. calmness, composure 3. unconcern, indifference
heavy 1. light, slight, small, trivial, yielding 2. bright, optimistic, hopeful
hectic calm, peaceful, uneventful
hedge meet, face, confront, be decisive
heed ignore, disregard, avoid, disobey
hefty light, small, slight, weak, feeble
help hinder, hamper, obstruct, impede
herald ignore, conceal, usher out
heroic unheroic, cowardly, scared
hesitate hurry, hasten, proceed
hide uncover, reveal, expose, disclose
hideous beautiful, fair, handsome, attractive
high 1. low 2. unimportant, nondescript 3. low-pitched, weak
hilarious unhappy, sad, gloomy, depressing
hill vale, dale, valley, hollow, depression
hinder help, aid, assist, support
hindmost first, foremost

hire dismiss, discharge

hitch 1. unfasten, untie 2. help, solution

hoard spread, distribute, scatter, spend

hold 1. release, free 2. reject, lose, forfeit 3. disbelieve, deny

holiday work, employment, job

hollow 1. solid, full 2. sincere, frank, unpretentious 3. mound, hill

holy unholy, sacrilegious, defiled, profane

homely comely, attractive, pretentious, sophisticated

honest dishonest, untruthful, deceitful

honor dishonor, disgrace, shame, disrepute

hoodwink enlighten, undeceive, inform

hope be resigned, be pessimistic about, despair

hopeless hopeful, promising, optimistic

horrible pleasing, pleasant, attractive, charming

horrid pleasing, attractive, agreeable

horrify calm, soothe, please, charm, captivate

hospitable unfriendly, unsociable, unneighborly

host 1. few, small number/quantity 2. customer, guest

hostile friendly, amicable, hospitable

hot 1. cold, frigid, icy 2. indifferent, slow

huge small, tiny, miniature, minute, microscopic

human inhuman, brutal, cruel, pitiless

humane inhumane, brutal, cruel, without pity/mercy

humble proud, vain, arrogant, haughty

humor 1. tragedy, seriousness 2. disagree with

hungry well-fed, replete, full

hunt escape, flee, fly

hurl catch, grab, clutch, clasp, seize, hold

hurry slow down, go slow, falter

hurt heal, cure, aid, assist, protect, preserve

hypocritical sincere, honest, frank, candid, straightforward

icy 1. warm, hot, heated 2. friendly, sociable

ideal imperfect, unsatisfactory'

identical different, unlike, dissimilar, unequal

idiotic sensible, sound, reasonable, rational

idle active, busy, occupied, engaged

ignite extinguish, put out, snuff

ignorant knowledgeable, educated, well-informed

ignore notice, observe, heed

ill 1. well, fit, healthy 2. good, lucky, fortunate

illegal legal, lawful, permissible, allowed

illness health, vigor, fitness

illogical logical, reasonable, sensible, rational

illuminate darken, shade

illusion reality, fact, truth, actuality

imaginary real, factual, not abstract

immediately soon, shortly, presently, later

immense small, little, tiny, minute

immerse emerge, draw/pull out

immortal mortal, impermanent, transient

immovable 1. movable, mobile, portable 2. irresolute, wavering

impart withold, suppress, conceal

impartial partial, biased, unfair, prejudiced

impatient patient, calm, composed

impede impel, propel, help, assist

imperfect perfect, complete, flawless, unblemished

impertinent polite, courteous, respectful

impetuous cautious, thoughtful, mindful, prudent

implore give, grant, allow, permit

impolite polite, courteous, civil, mannerly

important unimportant, trivial, unnecessary

impose take off, remove, abolish

imposing unimposing, unimpressive, ordinary, commonplace

impressive unimpressive, ordinary, insignificant

impromptu prepared, planned, rehearsed

improper proper, correct, becoming, suitable

improve worsen, become inferior, deteriorate

imprudent prudent, wise, cautious, thoughtful

impudent polite, courteous, respectful

impulsive careful, cautious, restrained, prudent

impure pure, unadulterated, clean

inadequate adequate, suitable, sufficient

inappropriate appropriate, suitable, fitting

incessant irregular, intermittent, periodic

incompetent competent, capable, proficient

incorrect correct, right. accurate, exact

increase decrease, lessen, reduce, fall

incredible credible, acceptable, easy to believe

indecent decent, proper, correct, seemly

indefinite definite, certain, sure

independent dependent, obedient, subordinate
indifferent interested, concerned, bothered
indirect direct, straight, nearest
indispensable inessential, unneccessary, not required/needed
indistinct distinct, clear, plain, definite, certain
industrious idle, lazy, inactive, unoccupied
ineffective effective, useful, appropriate
inevitable doubtful, uncertain, unsure
inferior 1. above, on top, elevated 2. superior, first class, better
infinite finite, limited, definite
infirm 1. firm, stable 2. strong, well, healthy
inflame extinguish, put out
inflate deflate, contract, shrink, decrease
inform not divulge, conceal, hide, learn
infrequent frequent, numerous, regular
infuriate calm, soothe, placate, mollify
ingenious foolish, untalented, simple
inhabit desert, vacate, abandon, forsake
inhuman human, humane, kind, compassionate
injure protect, preserve, help, assist
innocent guilty, blameworthy, condemned
inquire reply, retort, answer
inquisitive incurious, indifferent
insecure secure, safe, guarded, protected
insignificant significant, important, consequential
insolent polite, courteous, respectful
instant delayed, slow, tardy, belated
instruct learn, obey, follow
insufficient sufficient, adequate, enough
insult compliment, commend, praise
intact damaged, injured, broken, defective
intelligent stupid, dull, backward, retarded
intentional accidental, unprepared, unplanned
intricate simple, easy, uncomplicated
invalid 1. valid, acceptable, applicable 2. fit/healthy person
irate calm, pleased, contented, serene
irksome easy, pleasant, agreeable, interesting
irritable calm, placid, unruffled, serene
irritate calm, soothe, please, pacify
jagged smooth, even, level
jam release, free, liberate, unpack
jealous content, trusting, loyal, tolerant

jeer applaud, praise, compliment, commend
jerk push, shove, thrust, poke, jab
jittery calm, relaxed, composed, confident
join disunite, untie, detach, disconnect
jolly sad, solemn, serious, gloomy, surly
joy unhappiness, sadness, misery, gloom
jubilant unhappy, sad, miserable, downcast
jumble order, put in order, arrange, sort out
just unjust, unfair, partial, biased, improper, unrighteous, unbecoming
justice unfairness, partiality, bad treatment
juvenile adult, grown-up, mature person
keen 1. uninterested, indifferent, inactive, unenthusiastic 2. dull, obtuse, insensitive
keep throw away, discard, disobey, ignore
kill spare, protect, safeguard, preserve
kin strangers, foreigners, aliens
kind unkind, mean, spiteful, harsh, cruel
know misunderstand, not comprehend/realize, be unversed in/ignorant/unaware
knowing uninformed, ignorant, unaware
knowledge ignorance, lack/shortage of information
labor ease, comfort, leisure, pleasure
laborious easy, simple, light, lazy
lack abundance, adequacy, wealth
lag hasten, hurry, accelerate
lame 1. uninjured, whole 2. satisfactory, adequate, acceptable
land embark, board, go aboard
large small, little, tiny, wee, minute, miniature
last 1. first, foremost, primary, initial, opening 2. fade away, disappear
lasting temporary, transient, short-lived
late 1. early, prompt, immediate 2. present, living, existing
laugh cry, weep, sob
laughable sad, sorrowful, serious, solemn
lavish plain, simple, poor, cheap, inexpensive
lawful unlawful, illegal, illicit, illegitimate
lawless law-abiding, orderly, well-conducted
lax strict, rigid, firm, reliable
lazy active, busy, industrious, diligent
lead 1. mislead, misguide 2. follow, support
leader follower, supporter, adherent

lean 1. straighten up, become erect 2. fat, stout, plump, obese

learned ignorant, uneducated, illiterate

learning ignorance, illiteracy

leave 1. return, enter 2. prohibition, ban 3. work, employment

left right, right-hand, right-hand side

legal illegal, unlawful, illicit, illegitimate

legend fact, truth, actuality, history

legendary factual, true, actual, historical

legitimate 1. illegitimate, unlawful, illicit, unlawful 2. false, pretended, counterfeit

leisure work, job, employment

lengthen shorten, decrease, reduce, contract

lenient strict, rigid, firm, severe

lessen increase, extend, expand

let prevent, prohibit, ban

level 1. perpendicular, inclined, uneven, irregular 2. erect, build

liberate arrest, seize, hold, detain

lie 1. stand, sit 2. tell the truth, be honest

lift 1. lower 2. hindrance, obstruction

light 1. dark, dull, shady, unlit, unilluminated 2. strong, robust, heavy, weighty

lighten 1. darken, shade 2. increase, enlarge, make greater

like 1. dislike, disapprove of, detest, abhor 2. not alike, dissimilar, unlike

limit increase, extend, raise, allow, encourage

limp stiff, rigid, firm, erect

linger hurry, hasten, be quick/swift

link disconnect, uncouple, unfasten

list straighten up, become erect

listen ignore, disregard, not attend

listless active, energetic, vigorous

little large, big, great, huge, enormous

live 1. die 2. inactive, slow 3. extinguished, harmless, dead

lively 1. inactive, slow, sluggish, lethargic 2. sad, gloomy, melancholy, unhappy

loathe like, love, adore, admire, cherish

lofty 1. low 2. humble, simple

loiter hurry, hasten, be quick/swift

lonely crowded, accompanied

long short, brief, abrupt, immediate

look ignore, disregard

lose find, discover, retrieve

lot few, several, not much/many

loud quiet, silent, soft, faint, subdued

love dislike, loathe, hate, abhor

lovely plain, simple, ugly, unattractive, displeasing

loyalty disloyalty, infidelity, inconstancy

lucky unlucky, unfortunate, ill-fated

lull irritate, aggravate, anger, excite, stimulate

lustrous dim, dull, dark, unpolished

luxuriant meager, sparse, slight, poor

luxury need, want, poverty

macabre pleasing, beautiful, lovely, charming

mad 1. sane, sensible, rational 2. calm, composed

magnificent ordinary, commonplace, insignificant

magnify reduce, minimize

maid matron, married woman

maim preserve, guard, protect, spare

main lesser, less important, secondary

maintain 1. abandon, desert, disown 2. deny, disclaim

majestic undignified, ordinary, common, meek, plebeian

major minor, lesser, smaller, inferior, junior

majority minority, lesser/smaller part

make 1. unmake, destroy 2. discourage, dissuade

malady 1. remedy, cure 2. good health

male female, feminine, womanly, ladylike

mammoth small, little, tiny, miniature, minute

man female, woman, lady

manage mismanage, misdirect, disorganize

manageable unruly, undisciplined, wild, untamed

manhood childhood, youth

mankind womankind

manly feminine, womanly, ladylike

manners misconduct, discourtesy, incivility

manual mechanical, by machine

manufacture dismantle, destroy

many few, several, rare, infrequent

margin center, middle, midpoint

marine land, terrestrial

mark 1. clean, renovate, clear 2. ignore, disregard

maroon rescue, save, deliver

marry divorce, untie, disunite

marvelous ordinary, commonplace, unimpressive

masculine feminine, female, womanly, ladylike

mask reveal, disclose, expose, uncover

mass small quantity/amount, shortage, scarcity, paucity

massacre preserve, protect, spare

master 1. slave, servant 2. pupil, scholar, student 3. surrender, yield, give in

mastery inferiority, slavery, bondage

match 1. be dissimilar, disagree 2. inferior

material unreal, unsubstantial, irrelevant, abstract

matt smooth, flat, shiny

matter be irrelevant/unimportant/insignificant

mature unripe, young, immature

maximum minimum, smallest, least, lowest

maybe certainly, definitely, positively

meager ample, abundant, plentiful, copious

mean 1. ample, abundant, plentiful, sufficient 2. refined, kind, generous

meaning nonsense, unimportance, insignificance

meaningless purposeful, sensible, rational, logical, significant, meaningful

meddle ignore, avoid, disregard

meek harsh, arrogant, haughty, majestic

meet 1. avoid 2. dismiss, disperse 3. fail

melancholy happiness, joy, gladness, merriment

mellow unripe, immature, imperfect

member non-member, outsider

memorize forget, put aside

menace protect, preserve, help, support

mend break, damage, deteriorate

mention conceal, hide, ignore, disregard

mercy harshness, cruelty, brutality

merge separate, divide, come/go apart, disunite

merry unhappy, melancholy, cheerless, dreary

mess order, neatness, tidiness

method disorder, disorderliness, untidiness

methodical disorderly, unsystematic, without purpose

middle outside, exterior

might weakness, gentleness, meekness

mild 1. severe, harsh, unkind 2. cold, stormy

military 1. civilian, civil 2. naval

mind 1. neglect, disregard, ignore 2. forget 3. approve of, commend

mindful unmindful, inattentive, unheedful

miniature big, large, huge, enormous

minimum maximum, most, largest, highest

minor major, larger, greater, senior, superior

minority majority, greater/larger part

minus plus, with, additional to, positive

minute very/extremely big/large, enormous

miraculous ordinary, usual, commonplace

mirth sadness, melancholy, gloominess, unhappiness, misery

mischief 1. good conduct/behavior 2. protection, care

misconduct good conduct/behavior, order

miserable happy, gay, jolly, glad, gleeful

misfortune good fortune/luck, success

miss 1. notice, observe, hit 2. mistress, Mrs.

mix separate, segregate, part

mobile immobile, inactive, immovable, not portable

mock 1. real, genuine, actual 2. cheer, applaud, praise, commend, approve

model unmake, misshape, deform

moderate 1. unreasonable, extreme, fanatical 2. increase

modern old, ancient, old-fashioned, out-of-date, obsolescent

modest bold, extravagant, vain, conceited

moist dry, arid, dehydrated

molest comfort, console, protect, defend, help, assist

moment 1. age, long time, eternity 2. unimportance, insignificance

monarch subject, follower, subordinate

monotonous irregular, interesting, exciting

monster tame animal, kind/kindly/humane person

moody calm, composed, unruffled, phlegmatic

mope be content/cheerful/spirited

moral immoral, bad, unethical, dishonorable, dishonest, disgraceful, disgusting

motion inaction, inactivity, immobility

motionless active, moving, shifting, mobile, not still/stationary

mount 1. go/come/climb down, descend
2. hollow, valley, depression

mourn rejoice, exult

move 1. leave untouched 2. return 3. remain, halt, pause, stand still

multiply decrease, reduce, diminish, lessen

murder preserve, protect, spare

musty new, fresh

mutiny obey, serve, follow

mystery solution, answer, evidence

nag praise, applaud, commend, soothe

naked clothed, covered, dressed

narrow 1. wide, broad, thick, spacious, unlimited 2. impartial, broadminded

nasty pleasant, nice, agreeable, inoffensive, clean, unpolluted

native unnatural, civilized

natural affected, sophisticated, pretentious, abnormal, unusual

naughty good, well-behaved, polite, obedient, dutiful

near 1. far, distant 2. unrelated, disconnected

neat 1. untidy, unclean, slovenly 2. unskillful 3. impure, adulterated

necessary unnecessary, inessential

need 1. plenty, abundance, luxury 2. own, hold, possess

needy rich, prosperous, wealthy, affluent

negative positive, definite, correct

neglect care for, maintain, look after, preserve, remember

neglectful careful, thoughtful, considerate, attentive

nerve fear, cowardice, apprehension

nervous calm, composed, tranquil, bold, brave, resolute

net 1. release, free, liberate 2. gross

neutral partial, biased, prejudiced

new 1. old, out-of-date, obsolescent, familiar, previously known 2. previous, earlier

next 1. preceding, previous, prior, recent 2. at a distance, away from

nice 1. nasty, unpleasant, unfavorable, bad, disagreeable, unfriendly, ugly 2. inexact, inaccurate

nimble awkward, ungainly, slow, lethargic, dull

noble 1. ignoble, unworthy, dishonorable, mean, undignified, inferior 2. peasant, serf

nobody 1. somebody, someone, some person 2. person of importance/consequence

noise quiet, peace, stillness, silence

none some, someone, somebody, something

nonsense sense, logic, reason, sanity, wisdom

normal abnormal, irregular, unnatural, unusual,

notable undistinguished, obscure, unknown, unimportant

note 1. insignificant; unimportant 2. ignore, overlook, disregard, miss, not observe

notice ignore, disregard, miss

nourish starve, deprive, feed inadequately

novel old, out-of-date, unoriginal, common, ordinary, mediocre

novice professional, expert, master, specialist

nude clothed, dressed, covered, unexposed

nuisance help, assistance, helpful/inoffensive person

numerous few, several, not many

nutritious unwholesome, weakening, injurious

obedient rebellious, unyielding, undisciplined, disorderly, unruly, defiant

obey disobey, disregard, ignore

object approve, agree, consent, allow

oblige disoblige, hinder, hamper, obstruct

obscure 1. bright, clear, plain, distinct 2. notable, famous, distinguished, celebrated

observant 1. inattentive, careless, incautious, unwary 2. disobedient, defiant

observe 1. miss, overlook, ignore 2. disobey, break, violate, defy

obstacle help, aid, encouragement

obstinate yielding, submissive, obedient

obstruct help, aid, assist, support

obtain lose, return, forfeit, give up, spend

obvious obscure, unapparent, uncertain, indefinite

occasional frequent, regular, common

occupy leave, quit, abandon, desert, forsake, evacuate

odd 1. even, regular, uniform 2. normal, usual

odious nice, pleasant, pleasing, agreeable, charming, inoffensive

offend please, charm, oblige, satisfy, help, assist

offensive pleasing, charming, obliging, helpful

offer 1. take accept 2. levy, tax, duty

official unofficial, unauthorized

old 1. new, recent, modern, current, up-to-date 2. young, youthful 3. original, novel, stylish

omit include, insert

onward backward, backwards, rearward, rearwards, behind, to the rear

open 1. shut, closed, covered, hidden, undisclosed 2. hypocritical, insincere 3. end, finish, conclude

opening 1. barrier, bar, barricade 2. ending, final, concluding, closing, last

opponent ally, friend, companion, mate, assistant

opportune inopportune, inconvenient, badly-timed

oppose help, assist, support, follow, obey

opposite same, alike, like, similar

opposition help, assistance, support, cooperation

optimistic pessimistic, unhopeful

order 1. obedience, acceptance 2. disorder, untidiness, disarray

orderly 1. disordered, chaotic, untidy 2. unruly, rebellious, disobedient

ordinary unusual, uncommon, odd, queer, strange, extraordinary

origin end, finish, result

originate end, finish, terminate, demolish, destroy

outlet inlet, entrance, way in, access

outside 1. inward, inwards, within 2. interior, internal, inside

outstanding inferior, unexceptional, obscure, ordinary, usual, commonplace

outward 1. inward, inwards, within 2. internal, on the inside

over 1. under, below, beneath 2. less/fewer than 3. begun, started, commenced, opened

overcome submit, surrender, yield, give in

overlook notice, note, heed, mind

overpower submit, surrender, yield, give in

overthrow be overthrown/abased, surrender

overwhelm submit, surrender, yield, give way

owe be in credit/a creditor

own 1. give up, hand over, forsake, abandon 2. deny, disclaim, dispute

pagan enlightened, believer

pain pleasure, enjoyment, contentment, tranquillity, peace

pair disunite, uncouple, untie

pale bright, brilliant, radiant, vivid, intense

paltry important, significant, worthwhile, essential

pamper punish, chastise, discipline, deny, deprive

pandemonium order, calm, tranquillity, peace, quiet, silence

panic calm, composure, peace, courage, order

parade dismiss, disperse

parched wet, moist, damp, soaked, sodden, humid

pardon 1. blame, accuse 2. punish, penalize

part 1. whole, total 2. join, unite 3. return

particular 1. indistinct, not exclusive, inessential 2. incautious, careless, not fastidious

partner opponent, competitor, rival, enemy

pass 1. follow, succeed, chase 2. receive, take 3. disallow, forbid, prohibit, ban 4. barrier

passion calm, composure, tranquillity, indifference, nonchalance

pastime work, employment, business

patient impatient, incautious, hasty, rash, impetuous, intolerant

pause continue, carry on, proceed, advance

pay 1. charge, levy 2. receive, accept

peaceful noisy, clamorous, tumultuous, frenzied, chaotic

peak bottom, base, lowest part, foundation

peculiar normal, usual, ordinary, commonplace

penalty prize, reward, gift, present

perfect imperfect, incomplete, defective, faulty, blemished, inglorious, not absolute

peril 1. safety, security 2. caution, care

perish 1. survive, live, exist, endure 2. keep fresh

permanent impermanent, transient, temporary, brief

permit prohibit, disallow, forbid, ban, bar, deny, refuse, prevent

perpendicular flat, level, horizontal

perpetual impermanent, transient, temporary, brief

perplex assure, convince, enlighten, instruct

persecute please, charm, encourage, support, assist

persevere 1. give in, yield, hesitate 2. cease, stop

persist 1. give in, yield, hesitate 2. cease, stop

personal 1. not private 2. public, impersonal

persuade discourage, dissuade, deter

pest 1. help, assistance 2. helpful/harmless/inoffensive person

et 1. wild animal 2. tease, pester, annoy, irritate

etty 1. important, significant, essential, great urgent, worthwhile 2. generous, tolerant

ick 1. reject, refuse, disallow 2. spread, scatter, disperse

iece total, whole, complete quantity/amount

ile disperse, broadcast, scatter, spread

itiful cheerful, gay, contented, pleasing, attractive, charming

ity 1. indifference 2. cruelty, brutality, severity

lace displace, move, transfer

lague help, assist, soothe, placate, pacify

lain 1. decorative, fine, grand, magnificent, sophisticated 2. obscure, complicated, indistinct 3. uneven, undulating

lan disarrange, unsettle, disorder

lant 1. uproot 2. displace, remove, pick/pull up

lants animals, fauna, animal-life

lay work, employment, seriousness, solemnity

lead grant, allow, permit, concede

leasant unpleasant, ugly, unattractive, disagreeable, drab

lease displace, offend, irritate, bother, trouble, discomfort

lentiful scarce, sparse, meager, slender

luck 1. return, put down 2. cowardice, timidity

lump thin, lean, slender, small, slight

lunge 1. emerge, come out 2. withdraw, pull back

lolish make dull/lusterless

lolite impolite, discourteous, uncivil, rude, bad-mannered, unmannerly

loor 1. rich, wealthy, prosperous, luxurious 2. fertile, fruitful 3. superior, superb

lopular unpopular, unwanted, disliked

lortable immobile, immovable, stationary, fixed

lortion whole, all, full amount/quantity

lositive negative, indefinite, uncertain, unsure

lossess hand over, forsake, abandon, relinquish, give up

lossibly certainly, decidedly, definitely

lostpone 1. cancel 2. bring back/closer/nearer

loverty riches, wealth, prosperity, abundance, affluence

lower weakness, feebleness, inability

practical 1. useless, pointless, futile, empty, ineffective 2. unskilled, unskillful, inefficient

praise blame, condemn, accuse, decry, deride, jeer

preceding following, succeeding, subsequent, later

precise inexact, inaccurate, incorrect, erratic, indefinite

prefer refuse, reject, decline

prejudice impartiality, fairness, tolerance

preliminary final, end, concluding

prepare disarrange, disarray, disorder

preposterous sensible, logical, reasonable, rational

presence absence, non-attendance

present 1. absent, not here, away 2. take, receive, accept 3. past 4. future

presently later, in the future

preserve 1. spoil, destroy 2. discard, dispose of

press 1. pull, tug 2. discourage, dissuade, deter

pressing unimportant, insignificant, trivial, trifling, not urgent

presume doubt, disbelieve, disregard, ignore

pretty plain, unattractive, ugly

prevent allow, permit, encourage, assist, help

previous following, succeeding, subsequent, later

priceless worthless, valueless, without value, cheap, inexpensive

prime 1. second, secondary, lesser, subordinate 2. second-rate, inferior, poor, imperfect 3. later life, old age

principal lesser, minor, small, less important, unimportant, trivial

prisoner escapee, fugitive

private 1. impersonal, public, open 2. busy, crowded, congested

prize 1. dislike, abhor, loathe 2. punishment, penalty, forfeiture, fine

probable improbable, unlikely, uncertain, doubtful, impossible

problem 1. solution, answer 2. help, aid

proceed 1. finish, end, halt 2. retreat, retire, withdraw

proclaim disclaim, deny, gainsay

produce 1. destroy, demolish, eradicate 2. return 3. accept

profit loss

progress 1. go back, retreat, return 2. stop, halt 3. decrease, fall, decline

prohibit allow, permit, tolerate, consent to, grant

prolong shorten, reduce, lessen, decrease, limit

prominent obscure, unknown, unimportant, not famous/celebrated, unseen, insignificant, commonplace

promise refusal, denial, non-acceptance, disagreement

promising not hopeful, gloomy, discouraging, pessimistic

prompt 1. slow, delayed, late, tardy, neglectful, unmindful 2. discourage, dissuade, deter, hinder, hamper

propel repel, drive back, return

proper improper, incorrect, inexact, inappropriate, unsuitable, unbecoming, unseemly

prosper fail, lose, do badly, decline

protect 1. neglect, disregard 2. attack, ill-treat, abuse

protest agree, consent, accept, allow, permit

proud 1. humble, simple, homely, modest, meek, unpretentious, respectful 2. undignified, ignoble

prove disprove, contradict, deny, gainsay

prudent imprudent, unwise, incautious, careless, rash, impetuous

public private, personal, confidential

pull push, shove, thrust, drive

punish 1. excuse, pardon, forgive, overlook 2. reward, recompense

pupil teacher, tutor, instructor, coach

purchase sell, vend, retail, peddle, dispose of

pure 1. impure, adulterated, unclean, tainted 2. blameworthy, imperfect, sullied, ignoble, without virtue, unchaste

purify make unclean, sully, dirty, spoil, soil, taint, adulterate

pursue escape, flee, fly, avoid, dodge

push 1. pull, tug, yank, draw 2. discourage, dissuade, deter, hinder, hamper

puzzle enlighten, inform, instruct

qualified unqualified, inept, incompetent, incapable, untrained

quarrel agree, understand

quarry hunter, pursuer, predator

quash support, uphold, follow, assist, help

queer 1. ordinary, normal, usual, regular, not suspect/suspicious/questionable 2. well, fit, not sick/faint/indisposed

quell uphold, support, encourage, assist

query answer, reply, retort, response

questionable unquestionable, certain, sure, definite, agreed, proven

quick 1. slow, sluggish, lethargic, slothful, inactive 2. dull, stupid, unintelligent 3. patient careful, cautious, tolerant

quiet 1. noisy, audible, rowdy, clamorous, tumultuous, loud, excitable 2. active, obtrusive, garish, vivid

quit 1. return, go/come back, reoccupy 2. keep, retain, adopt 3. continue, carry on

quite incompletely, partially, partly

race slow down, linger, loiter, stroll

rack please, ease, relieve, alleviate

racket silence, quiet, calm, peace, serenity, tranquility

rage calm, composure, serenity

ragged neat, tidy, smart, elegant

raid 1. protect, defend 2. retreat, withdraw

rail praise, commend, applaud, approve

raise 1. drop, lower 2. decrease, lessen, diminish reduce 3. neglect, abandon 4. disperse, spread 5. calm, soothe

ramble 1. stay, remain 2. keep to the subject

range stay, remain

rank 1. disarrange, disarray, separate 2. scanty, sparse 3. gentle, mild

rapid slow, sluggish, lethargic

rare frequent, common, usual, typical

rascal noble/fine/virtuous person, hero, saint

rash cautious, careful, thoughtful, prudent

rather 1. greatly, manifestly 2. less truly

rattle 1. quietness, silence 2. assure, encourage

ravenous well-fed, satisfied, satiated

raw 1. prepared, cooked 2. experienced, trained 3. painless, insensitive 4. warm, fine

reedy 1. unready, unwilling, unprepared 2. slow, hesitant, reluctant

real unreal, false, sham, bogus, counterfeit

realize misunderstand, not comprehend, be unaware

rear 1. front, fore part, anterior 2. first, foremost 3. neglect, fail to train/educate

reasonable unreasonable, improper, unjust, unfair

rebel 1. obey, follow, support, adhere 2. follower, supporter

recall 1. forget 2. send out

eceive give, reject, lose, decline, refuse

ecent 1. former, old 2. succeeding, following

eckless cautious, careful, thoughtful, prudent

ecline sit up, stand

ecognize misunderstand, miss

ecollect forget, disregard

ecommend disapprove of, condemn

ecover 1. lose, mislay, drop 2. relapse, decline

ecreation work, labor, employment

educe 1. increase, enlarge 2. surrender, yield 3. strengthen

eflect overlook, ignore, disregard, neglect

efresh weaken, tire, exhaust

efuge trap, snare, pitfall, peril, danger

efuse accept, receive, take, acknowledge

egain lose, mislay, drop

egard 1. disregard, ignore 2. disrespect

egret rejoice, be glad/pleased/joyful

egular 1. irregular, impermanent 2. incorrect, improper, abnormal 3. erratic

eject accept, receive, take, get

elax 1. increase, tighten 2. strive, struggle, work

elease 1 catch, capture, seize 2. keep, retain, hold

eliable unreliable, disloyal, unfaithful

elieve hinder, frustrate, distress, upset, agitate

eluctant willing, keen, eager, ardent

ely distrust, mistrust

emain go/get/come away, leave, depart, quit

emark ignore, disregard, overlook

emarkable simple, plain, common, ordinary, normal

emedy harm, hurt, damage

emember forget, overlook, miss, neglect

emote near, close, adjacent, neighboring

emove 1. replace, return 2. place, set down, plant

epair damage, destroy, break, fracture

eplace remove, take away, displace

eply ask, demand, question, request

eport suppress, withhold, conceal

escue 1. lose, mislay, drop 2. capture, seize, imprison

eserve give up, lose, distribute, release

eserved 1. bold, sure, confident 2. released

esign retain, keep

resist submit, surrender, yield, give in

resolution indecision, hesitation

resourceful incompetent, inefficient, unimaginative

respect show disrespect, disregard, ignore

respectable dishonorable, indecent, not respected

responsible irresponsible, negligent, careless, thoughtless

restful uncomfortable, disturbed, unrelaxed

restless calm, peaceful, tranquil, placid

restore 1. remove, seize, take 2. damage, ruin, harm

restrain encourage, urge, persuade

restrict allow, permit, tolerate, sanction

result cause, origin, start, beginning

resume cease, end, finish, stop

retire 1. attack, advance, enter 2. arise, get up

retort ask, demand, question

return 1. take, obtain, get 2. retain, keep, hold 3. depart, go out, leave, quit

reveal conceal, cover, hide, mask

reverse 1. confirm, maintain 2. same side, obverse, face, front 3. victory, triumph, gain

revise ignore, disregard

revive 1. decline, relapse, deteriorate 2. die

revolt obey, follow, support, remain

revolting pleasing, attractive, charming

reward penalty, punishment, forfeiture

rich 1. poor, needy 2. infertile, barren 3. dull

riddle 1. answer, solution 2. manifestation

ridicule admire, praise, applaud, respect

ridiculous sensible, rational, reasonable, logical, proper, sound

right wrong, incorrect, improper, untrue, unfair, inappropriate

rigid loose, slack, lax, flexible, pliable, elastic

ripe unripe, immature, young

rise 1. sit, lie down, recline 2. descend, go downwards, fall, drop 3. decrease, lessen 4. end, finish 5. hollow, depression

risk security, safety, assurance

rival colleague, partner, ally, comrade

roam remain, rest, stay, stop

rob give, contribute, offer, return, replace

robust weak, feeble, frail, fragile, delicate

rogue upright/honest person, hero, saint

romantic unromantic, not fanciful, unimaginative

rot keep, preserve, conserve

rough 1. smooth, even, regular 2. calm, orderly 3. mild, gentle 4. polite, courteous, refined

round 1. square 2. straight, flat, level

rouse soothe, calm, placate, appease

routine irregular, unusual, exceptional, unofficial

row 1. agreement, conciliation 2. silence, quietness

rude polite, courteous, civil, respectful

ruin 1. restore, renew, refurbish 2. protect, improve

rumor factual/truthful/accurate story

run move/travel slowly/sluggishly, loiter, linger, stroll, walk

rush move/travel slowly/sluggishly

ruthless kind, gentle, merciful

sack 1. employ, engage, hire 2. protect, defend

sacred unholy, unconsecrated, unsanctified

sad happy, gay, gleeful, merry, joyful

safe 1. unsafe, insecure 2. unreliable

satisfactory unsatisfactory, inappropriate, inadequate

satisfy dissatisfy, displease, disappoint, depress, worry

saucy respectful, polite, courteous, civil

savage 1. tame, docile 2. civilized, considerate 3. calm, serene

save 1. seize, capture 2. distribute, scatter, spend 3. waste, be extravagant with

scamp 1. respectable person 2. do properly, face up to

scanty abundant, ample, plentiful, adequate

scarce abundant, plentiful, ample, sufficient

scare calm, comfort, assure, embolden

scatter 1. reap, pick, gather, collect, harvest 2. assemble, meet, congregate

scoff praise, applaud, congratulate

scold praise, commend, applaud, encourage

scorn admire, esteem, honor, respect

scrap 1. whole, total 2. retain, keep 3. become friends

scream whisper, sigh, speak softly, mutter

screen reveal, expose, show, exhibit

search 1. lose, mislay 2. find, recover

secret known, proclaimed, announced

section whole, total, all

secure 1. insecure, unsafe, unfastened, loose, unstable 2. return, replace 3. neglect

see 1. ignore, disregard 2. misunderstand

seize release, deliver, return

seldom often, frequently, on many occasions

select reject, refuse, decline, return

sell buy, purchase

send 1. retain, keep, withhold 2. return

senseless 1. sensible, wise 2. conscious, aware

sensible 1. senseless, foolish, stupid, absurd, ridiculous, silly 2. unconscious, unaware

separate undivided, connected, attached, together, joined, united

serene disturbed, ruffled, upset, excited

serious 1. frivolous, comic 2. happy, merry, gay 3. unimportant, trivial

set 1. displace, remove, uproot 2. soften, melt

settle 1. rise, ascend, fly off 2. disarrange

sever join, unite

severe 1. soft, easy, gentle, flexible 2. elaborate, sophisticated 3. mild, calm

shabby 1. well-dressed, smart, neat, tidy 2. kind, sympathetic, considerate

shady 1. bright, well-lit, sunny 2. honest, trustworthy

shake keep/remain still/rigid, freeze

sham real, true, genuine, authentic

shame honor, respect, praise, commend

shameless honorable, respectable, praiseworthy

shape misshape, deform, mutilate

share 1. keep, retain, withhold 2. abstain from

sharp 1. dull, blunt 2. gentle, mild, tender, insipid 3. unintelligent, slow-witted, stupid, inattentive, unwary

sheer 1. gradual, gentle 2. slight 3. thick, bulky

shelter reveal, uncover, expose, endanger

shield reveal, uncover, expose, endanger

shift remain/keep still/firm, rest

shine 1. tarnish, make/grow dull 2. dullness

shock please, delight, charm, comfort, soothe

short 1. long, lengthy, tall, extended 2. ample, abundant, plentiful, rich 3. courteous, polite

shortage abundance, sufficiency, wealth, surplus

shout whisper, speak quietly, mutter, moan

show cover, conceal, hide, mask, disguise

shred total, whole

shrewd foolish, obtuse, thoughtless, imprudent

shrill soft, faint, gentle, low-pitched

shut 1. open, unfastened, unlocked released 2. free, shy bold, impertinent, fearless, heedless

sick well, healthy, fit, sound

significant insignificant, unimportant, trivial

silent noisy, loud, rowdy, clamorous

silly sensible, sane, intelligent, wise, rational, reasonable, logical

simple 1. difficult, hard, complicated 2. elaborate, sophisticated 3. insincere, dishonest

sincere insincere, dishonest, not genuine, hypocritical

skillful unskilled, inexpert, untalented, incompetent, inefficient

slack 1. tight, taut, rigid 2. careful, diligent, quick, busy

slay preserve, protect, defend, spare

sleek dull, lusterless, coarse, drab

slender 1. wide, broad, thick 2. abundant, ample

slight 1. large, significant, important, severe 2. stout, strong, sturdy 3. praise, commend

slim 1. fat, wide 2. strong, great, good

slip correction, amendment

sly open, honest, sincere, straightforward

small big, large, significant, important

smart 1. untalented, dull, stupid, unwary 2. untidy, shabby, unfashionable 3. tender, mild, painless, easy

smooth 1. uneven, rough, coarse 2. restless, agitated

snatch return, replace, restore

sneer praise, applaud, commend, encourage

sob laugh, smile, grin, chuckle

sober gay, merry, undignified, drunk, intoxicated

soft 1. hard, solid, strong, rigid, stiff, unyielding 2. severe, harsh, strict 3. loud, high-pitched

solemn happy, gay, merry, undignified

solid 1. hollow, empty 2. soft, weak 3. unsound, unreliable

solitary 1. several, many 2. accompanied, crowded

soothe irritate, vex, annoy, disturb, agitate

sore 1. painless, insensitive 2. pleased, happy

sorrow happiness. joy, delight, comfort

sorry 1. happy, glad, delighted, pleased 2. impressive, pleasing, delightful

sound 1. quietness, silence 2. unsound, silly, foolish, ridiculous, absurd 3. unfit, unhealthy

sour 1. sweet, mild 2. cheerful, pleasant

source end, finish

space barrier, blockage, stop

spare abundant, ample, plentiful, generous

sparse ample, adequate, rank, thick

speed slowness, sluggishness, tardiness

splendid dull, inferior, unimpressive, not exciting

spoil 1. protect, preserve, retain, keep 2. thrive, flourish, grow

spread 1. gather, collect, pick/roll up 2. hide, conceal

squabble agree, concur, cooperate

squalid pleasing, pleasant, clean, lovely

start 1. stop, finish, end, terminate, conclude 2. return, go/come back

startle soothe, please, comfort, pacify

staunch disloyal, unfaithful, inconstant, unreliable

stay go, leave, depart, set off

steady unsteady, unstable, not firm, shaky

stern gentle, kind, friendly, considerate

stiff soft, limp, flaccid, movable

still 1. active, moving 2. loud, noisy

stir soothe, calm, quiet, pacify

stop 1. begin, commence, start, open 2. go, depart, return

store distribute, scatter, dispose of

story fact, truth

stout 1. thin, slender, lean, slight 2. weak, delicate, fragile 3. timid, afraid, cowardly

straight 1. bent, curved, crooked, uneven 2. untidy, incorrect 3. false, insincere, hypocritical

strange ordinary, normal, regular, familiar

strict gentle, kind, tolerant, easy-going

strong 1. weak, feeble, delicate 2. dull, dim, faint 3. fresh, pure

stubborn flexible, yielding

stupid sensible, intelligent, logical, rational

sturdy weak. feeble, delicate, frail, sickly

subdue surrender, yield, give in, submit

succeed 1. lose, fail, decline 2. precede, go before/in front

sudden slow, gradual, measured
suffer 1. avoid, overcome 2. forbid, disallow
sufficient insufficient, inadequate, not enough
suggestion command, order, instruction, directive
suitable unsuitable, improper, inappropriate, unbecoming
superb ordinary, commonplace, inferior, uninspiring
support abandon, forsake, hinder, burden
suppose know, understand, be certain/sure
sure unsure, uncertain, indefinite, doubtful
surly pleasant, agreeable, genial, friendly
surprise expectation, anticipation
surrender conquer, defeat, beat, subdue, suppress
suspicious certain, sure, trustworthy, reliable
sweet sour, bitter, acid, tart, malodorous, displeasing, disagreeable, unpleasant, obnoxious
swift slow, sluggish, gradual, tardy
sympathy disinterest, indifference, coldness
system disorder, confusion, mess, chaos
tactful tactless, indiscreet, undiplomatic, blundering
taint preserve, keep, clean, purify
take give, offer, present, donate, return, release
tale fact, truth
talent inability, incapability, incompetence
talkative silent, quiet, uncommunicative, taciturn
tall short, low, slight, squat
tame wild, savage, fierce, not domesticated
tasteful displeasing, inartistic, unstylish, inelegant
tasty tasteless, unsavory, bitter, tart, insipid
teach learn, study
tease please, charm, soothe, placate, pacify
tedious interesting, exciting, amusing, entertaining, appealing
tempt repel, disenchant, disillusion
tender 1. hard, rough, coarse, tough 2. harsh, unkind, unsympathetic 3. painless, easy
terminate begin, start, commence, open
terrible pleasing, pleasant, charming, attractive
terrific small, trifling, unimportant, insignificant
terrified calm, assured, serene, composed
terror courage, boldness, unconcern, indifference

thankful unthankful, ungrateful, thankless, unrewarding
thick 1. sparse, scanty, meager 2. thin, narrow, slender, slim, slight
thin 1. fat, stout, thick, wide, broad 2. sufficient, adequate, abundant, ample
think disbelieve
thorough incomplete, unsatisfactory, imperfect,
threaten placate, mollify, pacify, console
throw catch, hold, grab, snatch, trap
tidy untidy, disorderly, messy
tight loose, insecure, weak, elastic
timid bold, daring, brazen, brave
tiny big, large, great, huge, significant
tire refresh, invigorate, beguile, excite
tiresome refreshing, invigorating, stimulating, inspiring
toil ease, rest, relaxation, leisure
tolerate forbid, prohibit, disallow, ban
top bottom, base, foundation
torment please, comfort, ease, pacify
tough soft, weak, feeble, delicate, frail
tow push, shove, drive
trace lose, mislay, drop, conceal, hide
tragic comic, funny, amusing, happy
trained uneducated, unprepared
tranquil disturbed, bothered, noisy, violent
transform preserve, keep, maintain, retain
trap release, set free, liberate, rescue
treachery honesty, loyalty, faithfulness, trustworthiness, constancy
treat displease, upset, bother
tremble keep still/steady, be petrified
tremendous small, tiny, minute, insignificant
trick 1. enlighten, inform 2. be honest with
tricky 1. honest, open 2. easy, straightforward
triumph defeat, failure, loss
trivial significant, important, outstanding
trouble calm, quiet, pacify, console
true 1. untrue, false, bogus, counterfeit 2. unfaithful, disloyal, insincere
trust distrust, disbelief, doubt, suspicion
trustworthy unreliable, unfaithful, disloyal, dishonest, treacherous
truth untruth, dishonesty, fabrication, fiction, lie, falsehood

try give up, lose heart, neglect

ugly 1. beautiful, handsome, lovely, attractive 2. pleasant, safe

unable able, capable, empowered

unaware aware, alert, conscious, awake

uncertain certain, sure, definite, settled

uncivil civil, courteous, polite, respectful

unclean clean, untainted, unsullied, pure

uncomfortable comfortable, agreeable, easy, pleasing

uncommon common, ordinary, usual, regular

unconcerned concerned, bothered, worried, troubled

uncouth graceful, refined, elegant, courteous

uncover cover, hide, disguise, mask

undecided decided, certain, sure, arranged

underhand honest, truthful, sincere, straightforward

understand misunderstand, not grasp/realize/ perceive/comprehend

undeserved deserved, merited, earned

undiscovered discovered, found, revealed, disclosed

undisturbed disturbed, troubled, unsure, ruffled

undoubted doubtful, uncertain, unsure, deniable

unearth lose, mislay, conceal, hide

uneasy easy, comfortable, calm, serene

unequal equal, identical, equivalent, even

unequalled equalled, matched, surpassed, exceeded

uneven even, level, flat, straight, uniform

unexpected expected, anticipated, foreseen, prophesied

unfair fair, just, proper, impartial

unfaithful faithful, loyal, true, devoted

unfasten fasten, tie, bind, connect, unite

unfit 1. fit, suitable, appropriate 2. well, healthy

unfortunate fortunate, lucky, successful

unfriendly friendly, companionable, genial, sociable

ungrateful grateful, thankful, appreciative, obliged

unhappy happy, glad, contented, uplifted

uniform unequal, uneven, irregular, varied

unimportant important, great, famous, significant

unjust just, fair, impartial, proper, apt

unkind kind, sympathetic, considerate, generous

unknown known, understood, discovered

unlikely likely, probable, possible

unlucky lucky, fortunate, successful

unnecessary necessary, wanted, needed, required

unreasonable reasonable, sensible, logical, sane

unreliable reliable, dependable, trustworthy

unruly orderly, disciplined, obedient

unsatisfactory satisfactory, suitable, appropriate, pleasing

unskilled skilled, talented, expert, trained

untidy tidy, neat, trim, orderly

until from when, from the time when

untrue 1. true, correct, right, accurate 2. loyal, faithful, constant

unusual usual, ordinary, common, normal

unwise wise, sagacious, sensible, prudent

unworthy worthy, worthwhile, deserving, honorable

upright 1. flat, level, horizontal 2. dishonest

uproar quiet, peace, calm, order

upset 1. set, place, plant 2. console, please

urge discourage, dissuade, deter

urgent unimportant, trivial, insignificant

use 1. misuse, waste, maltreat 2. keep, retain

useful useless, pointless, futile, unhelpful

useless useful, helpful, profitable, effective

usual unusual, uncommon, rare, irregular

utmost nearest, closest, smallest, weakest

uttermost nearest, closest, smallest, weakest

vacant 1. filled, taken, occupied, reserved 2. alert, wide-awake, sensible, shrewd

vacate fill, occupy, return to

vagabond upright/respectable person, hero, saint

vague clear, distinct, plain, certain, sure, definite, unambiguous

vain 1. humble, meek, simple, shy, unpretentious 2. useful, purposeful, meaningful, sensible

valiant ungallant, afraid, cowardly, unheroic

valley hill, mount, mound, mountain

value unimportance, insignificance, demerit

vanish appear, become visible, materialize

vanquish surrender, submit, yield, give in

variety sameness, similarity

various few, not many

vast small, tiny, minute, miniature, insignificant

vend purchase, buy

verbal not spoken, written

versatile rigid, inflexible, limited

vertical flat, level, horizontal

vex soothe, console, please, pacify

vice virtue, morality, decency, goodness, respectability, rectitude

vicious virtuous, moral, chaste, decent, good, respectable, rightful, kind, considerate

victim slayer, pursuer, hunter, predator

victory defeat, failure, loss

view 1. indifference, lack of interest disregard 2. ignore, disregard

vigilant inattentive, unaware, incautious, unwary

vigorous weak, feeble, lifeless, dispirited, inactive,

vile good, moral, virtuous, righteous, noble, saintly, pure, worthy

villain good/moral/upright person, hero, saint

violate 1. protect, preserve, defend, respect, improve 2. obey, observe

violent gentle, calm, peaceful, peaceable

virile weak, inactive, unhealthy, unmanly

virtue vice, wickedness, evil, immorality, wrongdoing, sin, corruption, defect, blemish

visible invisible, unseen, indiscernible, unclear

vision 1. reality 2. lack of imagination/ foresight/forethought

vital unnecessary, unimportant, trivial, inessential

vivacious dull, inactive, lifeless, torpid

vivid dull, faint, feeble, colorless, drab

vocal unspoken, not voiced/said

void 1. full, occupied, useful, valid, binding 2. receive, accept, ingest

volunteer decline, refuse, deny

vouch deny, gainsay

vulgar refined, cultured, courteous, polite, dignified, well-bred

vulnerable invincible, unassailable, safe, secure

wait go, depart, leave, retire, quit

wander 1. remain, stay 2. keep to the point

wane wax, flow, increase, rise, strengthen

want abundance, plenty, wealth, prosperity, affluence

warn praise, applaud, commend

warp straighten, unbend, preserve, keep

wary incautious, unwise, unwary, imprudent

waste 1. care, economy, thrift 2. grow, flourish, wax 3. finished article, product

wasteful careful, economical, thrifty, provident

watch ignore, disregard, neglect, be unwary/ inattentive

waver be certain/sure/steadfast, stand firm

wax wane, weaken, diminish, sink, ebb

wayward normal, obedient, amenable, dutiful

weak 1. strong, robust, powerful, firm, forceful 2. steadfast, resolute, deep

wealth need, want, poverty, destitution

weary fresh, lively, vigorous, eager

weep laugh, smile, chuckle

weird normal, regular, usual, common

wet dry, parched, scorched, arid

white 1. black, dark, swarthy 2. dirty, soiled

whole 1. incomplete, divided, partial 2. unsound

wicked 1. virtuous, sinless, moral, pious, respectable 2. good, well-behaved

wide narrow, thin, slender, slim, lean, slight

wild 1. tame, docile, domesticated, civilized 2. cultivated

willful 1. unintentional, accidental 2. easygoing, obedient, amenable

win lose, fail, give in, yield, surrender, submit

wise unwise, silly, foolish, imprudent

withdraw advance, continue, proceed, go on

withstand yield, collapse under

wonderful uninspiring, unimpressive, ordinary, commonplace, unspectacular

work 1. unemployment, inactivity, idleness, laziness 2. play, leisure

worn 1. new, fresh, unused, well-kept, well-preserved 2. refreshed, invigorated

worry soothe, please, comfort, console

worship irreverence, disrespect

worthless worthy, esteemed, valuable, useful

worthy worthless, base, ignoble, dishonest

wound protect, defend, preserve, spare

wrath calmness, composure, gentleness

wreck protect, preserve, maintain, keep

wretched 1. happy, gay, merry, bright, cheerful 2. noble, worthy, respected

wrong 1. right, correct, proper, accurate, suitable 2. virtuous, moral, righteous, just 3. legal, lawful, legitimate

yank push, shove, thrust, poke, jab

yell speak quietly/softly, murmur, moan

yield 1. defeat, conquer, subdue, vanquish, overcome 2. receive, accept

young old, aged, elderly, adult, mature, grown-up
youngster oldster, adult, grown-up, mature person
youth 1. age, maturity 2. man

zeal indifference, lack of interest, disinclination
zest torpor, dullness, sluggishness
zip indifference, feebleness, laziness

Forming Opposites

The foregoing list includes most of the antonyms that are in common use. Some of the others may be formed by using *affixes* – *ab-*, *dis-*, *-ful*, *-less*, *in-*, *un-*, etc.

An affix that is attached to the front of a word is called a *prefix:* e.g., *dis-* in *disorder.*

An affix that is attached to the end of a word is called a *suffix:* e.g., *-less* in *careless.*

These affixes, with examples to show how they are used, are listed below. However, you must be cautious when using affixes, for they can sometimes be misleading, e.g., *disorder* is an antonym of *order,* but *discipline* is not an antonym of *'cipline'* – *'cipline'* is not a word. Similarly, *inconstant* is an antonym of *constant,* but *inhabit* is not an antonym of *habit,* though both *inhabit* and *habit* are words.

Prefixes

a-	moral, amoral
ab-	normal, abnormal
ant-	arctic, antarctic
anti-	climax, anticlimax
counter-	balance, counterbalance
dis-	approve, disapprove
extra-	ordinary, extraordinary
im-	possible, impossible
in-	gratitude, ingratitude
mis-	understand, misunderstand
non-	sense, nonsense
pro-	claim, proclaim
retro-	active, retroactive
un-	do, undo
under-	privileged, underprivileged

Suffixes

-ee	employer, employee
-er	drawee, drawer
-ful	careless, careful
-less	fearful, fearless

Archaic Words

Archaic means 'out-of-date,' or 'obsolescent.' Archaic words are out-of-date words, that is, words that were once in common use but which, nowadays, are either never used at all or are used only occasionally.

Some of the commoner archaic words that are still in occasional use are listed below. These words are generally encountered in poetry, both classical and modern, and stories and plays that were written several centuries ago. Archaic words abound in fables and fairy stories.

adieu	*n.*	good-bye, farewell
afar	*adv.*	at/to a distance, to a remote/distant land/place
alack	*adv.*	surprisingly, unexpectedly
ay	*n.*	yes, yea
aye	*adv.*	ever, always
bard	*n.*	poet, minstrel
betroth	*v.*	bind, promise to marry/wed
changeling	*n.*	elf-child (left by fairies)
chanticleer	*n.*	cockerel
childe	*n.*	knight, squire, page
childer	*n.*	children
cubit	*n.*	forearm-length, 50 centimeters
dam	*n.*	mother
dexter	*a.*	of/on the right-hand side
dost	*v.*	do
doth	*v.*	does
erstwhile	*adv.*	formerly
eve	*n.*	evening
farthing	*n.*	quarter of a penny
fealty	*n.*	duty, loyalty, obligation
gobbet	*n.*	piece, morsel, lump
goodly	*a.*	1. handsome, comely 2. gallant 3. large
gramophone	*n.*	record player
grist	*n.*	corn, malt
groat	*n.*	fourpenny piece/coin
hand	*n.*	10 centimeters
hither	*adv.*	here, to this place, in this direction
howbeit	*adv.*	nevertheless, for all that
joust	*n.*	just, knightly combat
lackaday	*adv.*	grievously, sadly
lea	*n.*	meadow, grassland
league	*n.*	about five kilometers
leech	*n.*	physician, doctor
lilliputian	*a.*	small, little, miniature
linden	*n.*	lime, lime tree
lo	*int.*	look, see, behold
marconigram	*n.*	telegram
methinks		I think. It seems to me.
morn	*n.*	morning
nay	*adv.*	no, not
oft	*adv.*	often, frequently
peradventure	*adv.*	perhaps, if, lest
perchance	*adv.*	maybe, possibly
physic	*n.*	medicine
pied	*a.*	multicolored, variegated
plenteous	*a.*	plentiful, abundant, ample
Reynard	*n.*	fox
russet	*a.*	1. reddish-brown 2. rustic, homely
sinister	*a.*	of/on the left-hand side
sire	*n.*	father
sirrah	*n.*	sir
swain	*n.*	lover, suitor (male)
thee	*pron.*	you
thine	*pron.*	yours
thither	*adv.*	there, yonder, to that place
thou	*pron.*	you
thy	*a.*	your
tidings	*n.*	news, information
trice	*n.*	moment, second
troth	*n.*	truth, honesty, constancy
tryst	*n.*	meeting, appointment
twain	*n.*	two
welladay	*adv.*	grievously, sadly
whatso	*a.*	whatsoever, whatever
whither	*adv.*	where, to what place
wilt	*v.*	will
wireless	*n.*	radio
without	*conj.*	unless
	adv.	outside
ye	*pron.*	you
yea	*n.*	yes, ay
yon	*a.*	yonder, distant

Foreign Words and Phrases

Many English words are of foreign origin. For example: *spirit, spiritus (Latin); jealous, jaloux (French)*. Many of the foreign words and phrases listed below are in common use but have not yet been fully accepted into the English language. They are usually printed in italics.

Abbreviations used: *Arab.* Arabic, *Chin.* Chinese, *Fr.* French, *Gael.* Gaelic (Scottish or Irish), *Ger.* German, *Gk.* Greek, *Hind.* Hindustani, *It.* Italian, *Lat.* Latin, *Sp.* Spanish, *f.* feminine, *m.* masculine.

ad hoc (Lat.) special, immediate, for a particular occasion

ad infinitum (Lat.) indefinitely, eternally

ad interim (Lat.) for the time being

ad libitum (Lat.) freely, without restraint, ad lib

affaire de coeur (Fr.) love affair, romance

aide-de-camp (Fr.) assistant, deputy

à la carte (Fr.) as per the menu

alma mater (Lat.) his/her/their old college

amour propre (Fr.) pride, vanity, dignity

ancien régime (Fr.) old order/former government

anno Domini (Lat.) the year of Our Lord, A.D.

ante meridiem (Lat.) before noon

au fait (Fr.) acquainted, knowledgeable

auf Wiedersehen (Ger.) goodbye, farewell

au pair (Fr.) mutual service

au revoir (Fr.) goodbye, farewell

badinage (Fr.) banter, raillery, chaffing

belles lettres (Fr.) literary writings/studies

bête noire (Fr.) pet dislike/aversion

billet-doux (Fr.) love letter

Blitzkrieg (Ger.) violent war/campaign

bona fide (Lat.) in good faith

bon-bon (Fr.) sweet, confection

bon mot (Fr.) witty remark/comment

bon voyage (Fr.) pleasant/safe journey

camaraderie (Fr.) comradeship

carte blanche (Fr.) freedom of action, free hand

char (Chin.) tea

chic (Fr.) smart, elegant, dainty

circa (Lat.) about (dates)

communiqué (Fr.) official message/bulletin

confrère (Fr.) confidant

cul-de-sac (Fr.) blind alley/road

cum (Lat.) with

débâcle (Fr.) downfall, collapse

début (Fr.) first appearance

décor (Fr.) system of decoration

Deo volente (Lat.) God willing

de rigueur (Fr.) as demanded by etiquette

de trop (Fr.) too much, superfluous

dhobi (Hind.) washerman, washerwoman

émigré (Fr.) political exile

en bloc (Fr.) all together, in one body

encore (Fr.) again, repeat, repetition

en masse (Fr.) all together, in one mass

en passant (Fr.) ii, passing, by-the-by

en route (Fr.) on the way

ennui (Fr.) boredom, disinterest

entrée (Fr.) 1. right to be admitted
2. first course (meals)

entre nous (Fr.) between ourselves, confidentially

ersatz (Ger.) substitute, artificial, synthetic

esprit de corps (Fr.) team spirit, cooperation

exempli gratia (Lat.) for example, e.g.

exeunt (Lat.) they go out

exit (Lat.) he/she goes out

fait accompli (Fr.) accomplished feat/deed

faux pas (Fr.) blunder, error

fiancé (Fr.) m. engaged man (marriage)

fiancée (Fr.) f. engaged woman (marriage)

finis (Lat.) the end

Führer (Fuehrer) (Ger.) leader

garçon (Fr.) boy, waiter, servant

gendarme (Fr.) policeman

hoi polloi (Gk.) the common people, plebeians

hors de combat (Fr.) out of the fight, disabled

hors-d'oeuvre (Fr.) relish, extra/savory dish

id est (Lat.) that is, i.e.

ilk (Gael.) family, kin, creed

kaput (Ger.) completely finished, destroyed

kismet (Arab.) fate, fortune, destiny

kudos (Gk.) fame, glory, recognition

mot juste (Fr.) the very/apt word

ne plus ultra (Lat.) first-rate, excellent

nom de plume (Fr.) pen-name, pseudonym

non compos mentis (Lat.) of unsound mind, insane

nota bene (Lat.) note well, N.B.

par excellence (Fr.) excellently, preeminently

pâté (Fr.) paste

patois (Fr.) dialect

poilu (Fr.) French soldier

post meridiem (Lat.) after noon

presto (It.) quick, quickly, suddenly

purée (Fr.) pulp

raconteur (Fr.) storyteller, narrator

réspondez s'il vous plait (Fr.) please reply

sang-froid (Fr.) calm, coolness, composure

Sassenach (Gael.) Saxon, Englishman

savoir-faire (Fr.) tact, diplomacy, discretion

siesta (Sp.) afternoon nap/sleep

tempus fugit (Lat.) time flies/passes quickly

terra frima (Lat.) firm ground, solid earth

tête-à-tête (Fr.) face to face, secretively

videlicet (Lat.) namely, that is to say, viz.

volte-face (Fr.) sudden reversal of opinion/attitude

Weltpolitik (Ger.) world/international politics